Fifth Edition

HUMAN RELATIONS
AND
POLICE WORK

LARRY MILLER
MICHAEL BRASWELL
EAST TENNESSEE STATE UNIVERSITY

WAVELAND
PRESS, INC.
Prospect Heights, Illinois

For information about this book, contact:
Waveland Press, Inc.
P.O. Box 400
Prospect Heights, Illinois 60070
(847) 634-0081
www.waveland.com

This edition is dedicated to our children:
Ryan and Casey,
Scott and Matt.

CONTENTS

Section I
Police and the Community   1

Cases Involving Police and the Community   9

Section II
Family and Crisis Intervention   **31**

Cases Involving Family and Crisis Intervention   41

Section III
The Police and Juveniles   **61**

Section IV
The Police and the Emotionally Distressed   **89**

Section V
Police Stress   **117**

Cases Involving Police Stress   125

Section VI
Police Ethics   **149**

Cases Involving Police Ethics 155

ACKNOWLEDGMENTS

We wish to thank our academic and professional colleagues and our students for their suggestions and support with this edition. We appreciate the assistance of graduate students Jackie Chapman, Mike Bush, Amy Lyons, and Kim Dodson, as well as Sharon Elliott, our departmental secretary.

Special thanks go to the following academic colleagues who helped make this a better book: Michelle Bennett, Central Washington University; Max Bromley, University of South Florida; Charles Dirienzo; Horry/Georgetown Technical College; Jay Gannett, Peninsula College; Ronald Tannehill, Washburn University; and Nancy Walzel, Lamar State College.

INTRODUCTION

The intention of this book is to provide persons with the opportunity to identify with the various roles of a law enforcement officer. The reader is placed in common law enforcement and police situations and is expected to make a decision based on his or her best judgement. The roles range from police patrol officer to chief; from small-town police departments to metropolitan police agencies. The reader should try to remember that police rank, department type, and state law may influence the situations represented. In cases where state law may have a bearing on the outcome of a given situation, the reader should attempt to apply his or her own state law.

The book attempts to emphasize the learning aspects of role playing, identification, and problem solving. No answers are necessarily wrong or right. It is hoped that each case will provide the impetus for open discussion concerning the situations presented as well as other similar situations encountered daily in the police and law enforcement profession.

It is the authors' hope that this book will be viewed as a collection of examples of common and not so common occurrences in police work which require an action or response by the individual officer. In this way, the reader can become the decision maker and can rely on his or her own personality, experience, knowledge, and common sense in order to alleviate the problems presented. The reader will be asked to make decisions regarding case situations by responding to several questions located at the end of each case. The reader will also have the opportunity to discuss how the police officer handled the situation and if the situation could have been treated differently by the officer. It should be noted that a procedure followed by an individual officer in one of the cases situations may have presented a problem in itself.

This book is divided into seven sections. Each section deals with a particular area of concern to law enforcement officers. The reader should note that there may be some overlapping of section topics. For instance, the section dealing with police and the community may also contain problems which concern the topics of the sections dealing with police and juveniles, and so on.

It is suggested that the reader complete each section by reading, answering, and discussing the questions presented for the cases. The reader may then determine if his or her solutions and decisions represent the preferred course of action for a given case.

Finally, it is the intention of this book to show that no two situations are alike in police work. Each situation calls for a fresh and creative approach. In short, law enforcement and police work are not simple black and white processes, but consist of an endless variety of shades of gray.

There have been several revisions made for this Fifth Edition. A number of cases have been replaced and others revised. Text material for each section has been updated to reflect new legal procedures and more current research. These changes reflect the suggestions the authors have received from colleagues, practitioners and students. Responses from other professors and students as well as empirical research on the experiential model has indicated that the learning process can be enhanced using an experiential case study approach. Changes in the current edition of this text attempt to build upon and expand the positive applications of using this approach to acquaint the reader with the many facets of the criminal justice experience.

Section I

POLICE AND THE COMMUNITY

Introduction

Police-community relations in the United States has been a growing concern of criminal justice practitioners for decades. Sociologists, psychologists, and a host of other professionals have offered theories, ideas, and potential solutions for poor police-community relations. There are several reasons why police-community relations are of vital concern to criminal justice practitioners. Elected law enforcement officials may view police-community relations as a means of reelection; the patrol officer may view police-community relations as a means of gaining respect; criminal investigators may utilize police-community relations as a means for obtaining information; and police administrators maintain police-community relations as a means of obtaining funding for department programs. Perhaps the most significant aspect of police-community relations is the context in which the police and the community can work together in an effort to reduce criminal activity and insure the safety of citizens.

During the previous decades of policing, the community has become separated from those persons that police. The police are expected by society and by members of their own profession to transcend the individuals they are sworn to protect and serve. Such a separation often creates an aura of mystique concerning the police profession from the community's viewpoint and a cautious attitude of police officers toward society. This separation of police and community may have been the result of technological innovations or the historically political and corruptive influences

1

concerning the police role; or changing social values and structures. Regardless of the reason, the fact remains that the police are at times not only combating the criminal element in a community but, in a sense, the community as well.

The Public's View of the Police

After decades of public neglect of the police officer's role in society, the onset of the late 1960s and early 1970s accented public visibility of the police. During this era of social unrest and political protest and confrontation, the police were conceived as members and enforcers of the "system." During this time, police-community relations became vitally important for the stability of communities confronted with social conflicts. The increasing visibility of the police in the community, which was reflected in the nation's press and media, prompted a wide variety of misconceptions regarding the police role. Many Americans began to view the police as being solely responsible for controlling crime—a view that still exists in some segments of the public.

Our basic law enforcement ideals and organizational structures were imported from England. The British police system has always maintained that the police are the public and the public are the police (Gaines and Cordner, 1999). The British police system contends that it is every citizen's obligation to help police his or her society, but certain citizens are set aside to do the job on a full-time basis. The police, in this way, assist all citizens in their job. Our police system has not adequately related the reality that the public are, in fact, the police. It is thought that when crime rates are high in a community, it is because the police are not doing their job, rather than that society has failed to some extent in their responsibilities.

The President's Commission on Law Enforcement recognized in the late 1960s that law enforcement as an occupation demanded a great degree of skill and intelligence (National Advisory Commission on Criminal Justice Standards and Goals, 1973). For decades the public has often been inclined to perceive the police as low-paid job holders with limited intelligence (Hodge, 1964). The fact that the public often seems to believe that the police are corruptible and influenced by political forces nurtures the suspicious and cynical attitudes of the community toward police officers (Fosdick, 1920). In order to alleviate those attitudes, the President's Commission on Law Enforcement helped establish the Law Enforcement Assistance Administration (LEAA), whose duty was to provide federal funding for police agencies in the United States. This agency increased the potential for professionalism regarding the police role. Increased training, education, salaries, and equipment for police officers and agencies were believed to give the police not only the tools required to combat crime, but a means to gain increased community support and respect. Although the LEAA was somewhat successful in providing the police with tools to combat crime, they did not gain the community support and respect for the police to which they had aspired.

Public attitudes toward police are embellished with fear and cynicism. American and many other Western societies seem to have always feared a strong police force. Fear and distrust of government authority, as symbolized by the police, is reinforced by the American culture of individual freedom. In recent years, American law enforcement has drawn national criticism in instances such as the Rodney King beating and the O.J. Simpson trial. With increasing distrust of federal law enforcement fueled by situations such as in Waco, Texas, Ruby Ridge, and the Freemen of Montana, anti-government militia and other groups have voiced their disapproval of federal law enforcement authority.

The media are always quick to publicize criticism of law enforcement and slow to offer praise. When a police officer risks his or her life to stop a criminal act, there is seldom substantial public recognition by the community. After all, the police were simply performing their duty. When police officers utilize authority to regulate behavior such as speeding, they are often condemned by many in the community. When police officers abuse their authority, they are chastised by the media and community. The wrongful acts of one or two police officers affect the image of all law enforcement officers.

The Police View of the Public

Police officers traditionally have been trained to be suspicious of all persons for the practical purpose of self-preservation. Such a suspicious attitude, reinforced by the public's attitude toward the police, can enhance the separation between the police and the community. Skolnick (1994) indicates that police officers possess personality traits unlike those of other professions. The combination of authority with danger as inherent elements of the police profession can isolate the police from the community. Such isolation allows the police to come together as a fraternal group with an "us against them" attitude. This type of solidarity creates a fraternal brother-sisterhood among police officers.

Because the police officer is continually occupied with anticipating potential violence, he or she develops a perception of those who are potentially dangerous. Police officers tend to stereotype certain individuals in society as symbolically dangerous based on their appearance and behavior (Skolnick, 1994; Crank, 1998). The tough-looking gang of youths on a street corner are scrutinized more closely by police officers on patrol than are the clean-cut group of boy scouts in the churchyard. However, the clarity of these situational perceptions is generally not as evident as depicted in the above example. Many police training films and exercises use scare tactics to illustrate to police officers that anyone can be dangerous (McNulty, 1994). Many police firearms training films illustrate that even the most innocent in appearance may be a potential assailant. While the police wear uniforms for recognition, the criminal is not as easily identified. Therefore, police officers may view suspiciously all persons unfamiliar to them, since their well-being may depend on such evaluation. Even off-duty police officers tend to socialize more readily with those in their respective or related profession.

Degrees of suspiciousness exist regarding the police view of the community. Police officers are inclined to view members of the higher social classes with less suspicion than those in the lower social strata. Members of the higher social classes generally possess a greater portion of money, power, and political ties and may appear more law-abiding. Because most police officers are generally derived from the middle class, they often tend to view those of the upper class with more respect. Upper-class sections of the community are not as apt to experience violent crimes as the lower-class areas. As a result, police officers may be more concerned with prevention of crimes such as burglary in these neighborhoods and less concerned with robberies, rapes, or assaults. Many police officers view the upper-class commission of crimes as those of social distinction such as murder, embezzlement, insurance fraud and the like. However, police officers on patrol in the lower-class sections of the community may anticipate crimes of violence and may be much more cautious of the people living there.

Police Use of Discretionary Decision Making

Wilson (1968) has identified three styles of police behavior in America: (1) legalistic style of policing; (2) watchman style of policing; and (3) service style of policing. The legalistic style of police behavior is concerned with those police officers who believe they are representatives of the law that they are sworn to uphold. Legalistic police officers refrain from judgment on the basis of the spirit of the law, trying to judge only whether a law is broken or followed. The legalistic style of policing could be equated with the "police officer who would give his own mother a ticket for speeding" philosophy. The watchman style of policing produces the opposite type of police officer. The watchman police style "overlooks" or ignores many violations of the law. These police officers, when not acting on a violation, are inclined to issue more warnings than tickets, and make fewer arrests. The service style of policing makes the greatest use of discretion. These police officers judge each situation on its own merits and base their decision to arrest on the well-being of the community. The service style of policing is a balance between the legalistic and the watchman styles of policing and has been suggested as providing one of the better forms of police-community relations (Wilson, 1999).

Police discretion has been defined as "the power to consider all circumstances and then determine whether any legal action is to be taken.

And, if so taken, of what kind and degree, and to what conclusion" (Breitel, 1960). Many citizens as well as police officers themselves feel police should not have the authority of discretion. These individuals feel it should be left to the court's discretion whether to inflict punishment upon a lawbreaker or ultimately to decide whether an offense has been committed. The conception of police officers as nonjudges is a misnomer (Crank, 1998). Police officers must utilize judgment daily in their job performance. Police discretion is used as an arrest or not-to-arrest judgment in the same manner a prosecuting attorney uses discretion in the plea-bargaining process. However, the prosecuting attorney and the judge usually do not have the power of discretion until the police officer makes the decision to arrest. The police officer's decision to arrest is the first step in the criminal justice process and is, perhaps, one of the most important steps. How the police officer utilizes his or her discretionary powers will affect the community view of the police and, to a large extent, the crime rates of the community (Price, 1979; Goldstein, 1993).

In a general sense, when the police take a legalistic approach to the control of crime and enforcement of the law, crime rates will rise because of increased arrests. When the police take a watchman approach to law enforcement, crime rates may decline because of decreased arrests. When the police take a service approach to law enforcement there may be less arrests, but the conviction rates should be higher and the types of crimes solved more serious in nature. The public is not inclined to report crime or cooperate with the police when they feel that the police are incompetent or more concerned with writing tickets than investigating crimes. When the police make visible efforts to cooperate with the public by using a service style of policing, the public becomes more cooperative. As a result, wise use of police discretion can enhance the police image and provide for better police-community relations.

Community Crime Prevention

The American police profession has traditionally been one of crime—apprehension—prosecution, rather than prevention. Although the early twenty-first century has brought increased attention to crime prevention, the concept is not new. The British police have, for decades, been concerned with the concept of investigating potential crime scenes before the fact.

Most people realize that the police cannot combat crime totally by themselves. The old British concept that the "police are the public and the public are the police" has brought new meaning to crime prevention programs developing in the United States. Poor economic conditions and increasing rates of violent and property crimes have traditionally encouraged public outcry toward crime. Liberal views toward the offender of the 1960s and 1970s have been replaced by more conservative views of crime control in the latter twentieth and early twenty-first centuries.

Crime prevention concepts, with goals to improve police-community relations and control crime, have evolved from the neighborhood watch and Operation Identification programs to more effective means of involving the community to help control crime. Many police departments now offer Citizen Academies, Anti-Drug Coalitions and Anti-Gang Coalitions, media advertisements and Crime Busters programs, and DARE programs in schools. Such programs actively recruit and encourage citizens to be a part of the crime control effort by the police. Such programs have shown success in improving police-community relations as citizens take back their neighborhoods from gangs and drug dealers (Office of Community Oriented Policing Services, 1997). Most citizens are willing and able to assist the police if asked. Therefore, it is vitally important that the police actively educate and recruit citizens to help control crime. This is one of the goals of community policing.

Community Policing

Community policing is touted as a new philosophy of policing, based on the concept that the police and the public must work together to solve community problems related to crime (Cordner, 1999; Thurman, Zhao, and Giacomazzi, 2001). A substantial number of police departments across the United States have implemented some form of community policing. Community policing is not a technique but a new definition of police values. Police managers are well aware that vast amounts of a police officer's time are spent on human and community problems, not just crime (Greene and Klockars, 1991; Crank, 1998). Rather than attempting to steer clear of a "social worker" image, the community policing concept encourages police officers to become helping professionals as well as crime fighters (Roberts, 1997). The community policing philosophy accepts the relativity of human problems and crime. Poverty, joblessness, personal frustrations and other social conditions create an atmosphere conducive to crime.

One of the characteristics of community policing is allowing all members of the police department to contribute to the operation of the department. Another is the sharing of decisions between the police and the community. It allows officers to get out of their patrol cars so they can maintain face-to-face contact with the people they serve. The community police officer serves as a generalist, a person who can tackle the problem of his/her own beat area and develop new ways to address community problems. Developing such a rapport with the community will both benefit the police in their primary mission as law enforcers and prevent the isolation that generally occurs between the police and the community (Thurman, Zhao, and Giacomazzi, 2001).

Community policing is a philosophy that views police officers as community problem solvers and not just crime fighters (Bauman, 2000).

Community police officers answer calls and make arrests, but they also do more. They provide innovative problem solving and a direct link between the community and local government. Some techniques that have been used or associated with community policing include: crime prevention programs, foot patrol, bicycle patrol, horse patrol, problem-oriented policing (POP), storefront policing, Total Quality Management (TQM), and Neighborhood Resource Officers.

One of the more promising strategies police use in collaboration with the community to identify and solve neighborhood problems is the SARA model (Thurman, Zhao, and Giacomazzi, 2001). This model is a four-phase process: scanning, analysis, response, and assessment. Scanning involves the identification of potential problems. Analysis is the information-collection phase used to determine the magnitude and causes of the problem. Response is the implementation of potential solutions. The assessment phase determines how effective the responses were in solving the problem. In all, the community policing philosophy is a fresh attempt to attain the British philosophy that "the police are the public and the public are the police."

Summary

In the past, the public has often viewed the police as inept, uneducated and corrupt political puppets, or as straight-laced tough guys with little compassion for their fellow citizens. Such views have, to some extent, been encouraged by the media, reinforced by social unrest, and promoted by police treatment of the general public. Police officers were expected to be a combination of lawyer, psychologist, soldier, and social worker. The police profession has, on many occasions, promoted mistrust, fear, and cynicism. In the same context, police officers have been trained to be suspicious of all, but to assume a role of objectivity and authority over those they serve. This has led to an unfortunate separation between the police and the community with the police in the middle, fighting criminal elements as well as community elements that criticize their actions. Only time will tell if this new philosophy of police work will be effective (Bauman, 2000).

With use of police discretion in enforcement of the law and encouragement of the community to help the police combat a common enemy, community support for police has increased. Crime prevention and community policing programs by police agencies have provided better police-community relations. Such programs can only be effective in creating better police-community relations when every police officer realizes that he or she must take the first step in showing the public that the police too are citizens who wish to assist the public in policing the community.

References

Bauman, M. P. (2000). "Police Productivity: A State of Mind, An Approach to the Job." *Police*, 24(1): 32–34.

Breitel, C. D. (1960). "Controls in Criminal Law Enforcement." *The University of Chicago Law Review*, 27 (Spring).

Cordner, G. W. (1999). "Elements of Community Policing." In L. Gaines and G. W. Cordner (eds.), *Policing Perspectives*. Los Angeles: Roxbury Publishing Co.

Crank, J. P. (1998). *Understanding Police Culture*. Cincinnati: Anderson Publishing Co.

Fisher, B. (1993). "What Works: Block Watch Meetings or Crime Prevention Seminars?" *Journal of Crime & Justice*, 16(1): 1–27.

Fosdick, R. B. (1920). *American Police Systems*. New York: The Century Co.

Gaines, L. K., and G. W. Cordner. (1999). *Policing Perspectives: An Anthology*. Los Angeles: Roxbury Publishing Co.

Goldstein, H. (1993). "Confronting the Complexity of the Policing Function." In L. Ohlin and F. Remingdon (eds.), *Discretion in Criminal Justice: The Tension Between Individualism and Uniformity*. Albany: State University of New York Press.

Greene, J. R., and C. B. Klockars. (1991). "What Police Do." In C. B. Klockars and S. D. Mastrofski (eds.), *Thinking About Police*, 2d ed. New York: McGraw-Hill.

Hodge, R. W. (1964). "Occupational Prestige in the United States, 1925–1963," *American Journal of Sociology*, 70 (November).

Lurigio, A., and D. Rosenbaum. (1994). "Community Policing." *Crime & Delinquency*, 40(3): 299–468.

McNulty, E. (1994). "Generating Common-Sense Knowledge among Police Officers." *Symbolic Interaction*, 17: 281–294.

National Advisory Commission on Criminal Justice Standards and Goals. (1973). *Police*. Washington, DC: U.S. Government Printing Office.

Office of Community Oriented Policing Services. (1997). *Community Policing*. Washington, DC: U.S. Department of Justice.

Price, R. P. (1979). "Integrated Professionalism: A Model for Controlling Police Practices." *Journal of Police Science and Administration* (March).

Roberts, A. R. (1997). *Social Work in Juvenile and Criminal Justice Settings*, 2d ed. Springfield, IL: Charles C. Thomas.

Skolnick, J. (1994). "A Sketch of the Policeman's Working Personality." In *Justice without Trial: Law Enforcement in a Democratic Society*, 3d ed. New York: Wiley.

Thurman, Q., Zhao, J., and A. Giacomazzi. (2001). *Community Policing in a Community Era*. Los Angeles, Roxbury Publishing Co.

Wilson, J. Q. (1999). "Dilemmas of Police Administration." In L. Gaines and G. Cordner (eds.), *Policing Perspectives: An Anthology*. Los Angeles: Roxbury Publishing Co.

CASES INVOLVING POLICE AND THE COMMUNITY

Case number one, "The Room at the End of the Hall," explores the problem of a possible sexual assault at a fraternity house and the intervention of university officials in dealing with the problem. The officer is faced with initiating the criminal justice process or allowing university officials handle the situation.

Case number two, "Hot Dog," involves a rookie police officer who has become a problem for a veteran officer attempting to "break him in." The rookie abuses his police authority by deliberately provoking citizens and handling situations in an aggressive manner. The veteran officer is faced with the responsibility of teaching the rookie the correct way of handling and interacting with people.

Case number three, "Park Place," examines how law enforcement in affluent neighborhoods may, in some cases, be applied differently and deferentially. Powerful community leaders, politicians, and their families may expect—and on occasion be granted—second chances that members of blue-collar or lower-income neighborhoods might not receive.

Case number four, "Liberty and Justice for All," is concerned with the profound social and cultural problems within the inner city. A police patrolman is transferred from a higher socioeconomic-class neighborhood patrol zone to an inner city patrol zone. The officer finds that different people are handled in different ways by the police. The officer finds himself making more arrests and becoming increasingly aggressive with individuals.

Case number five, "No Español," explores the stress of an officer deciding whether to take sides with a fellow officer in an unethical confrontation with non-English speaking individuals or report his actions to supervisors.

Case number six, "Community Policing: Network or Nightmare?" centers on the problems of making the community policing concept work. The commander of a community police center is faced with making changes in a department that holds to traditional police tactics.

Case number seven, "Officer Friendly—Unfriendly Neighborhood," deals with a police-community relations officer describing "neighborhood

watch" programs for an older neighborhood. The officer is faced with trying to explain the police position to a group of angry senior citizens.

Case number eight, "Hate Crimes," deals with a state trooper investigating an accident involving an interracial couple. Upon further investigation, the trooper finds that officers from the sheriff's department may
be involved in an assault upon the couple. The trooper must decide how
to best handle the situation.

CASE 1
THE ROOM AT THE END OF THE HALL

You have just showered and changed into civilian clothes. You think to yourself that, for a training officer, Sergeant Womack is all right. You have learned a lot from him during the last six weeks. Being a rookie police officer has gone much more smoothly than you thought it would. Finishing the last of your umpteenth cup of coffee, you can't help but overhear the sergeant and the afternoon shift dispatcher discussing several neighborhood calls complaining about a weekend fraternity party on Elm Street.

You say to the sergeant, "Sarge, I used to be a member of that fraternity when I was a criminal justice student at the university. I'd be happy to stop by on my way home and check it out. College boys can get a little rambunctious at times. I don't mind making a visit and getting them to quiet things down."

Sergeant Womack looks at the dispatcher and then turns to you.

"OK, Bill. Just be sure if there is any trouble, you call me pronto."

"You got it, Sarge," you respond, chuckling to yourself and remembering your rambunctious times at the fraternity house.

Parking your truck by the street in front of the fraternity house, you can see the situation is about what you expected. You quickly herd those persons partying in the yard into the house and announce to all, pulling your badge, to hold things down since the neighbors are complaining to the police. Your voice has a firm but friendly tone to it and the party goers, with a couple of minor exceptions expressed by several intoxicated brothers, generally comply with your request. You ask one fairly responsible-looking student in a fraternity sweatshirt where Ed, the organization's president, is, and he directs you to the last room on the right upstairs.

Entering the room, you observe seven or eight male students all watching some kind of activity in the corner of the room. Several are shouting encouragement while the rest are drinking beer and watching in silence. The observers are so enthralled with what is going on that they

11

don't even notice your presence as you work your way through the crowds to see what is going on. You stop in your tracks. There on a bed is a male student having intercourse with a girl. Next to the bed is another male student zipping his pants up. You cannot tell what state of mind the girl is in. She seems intoxicated and confused, and perhaps even somewhat frightened. Not exactly sure what to do, you pull your badge and tell everyone to step outside the room and not leave the house. You stop Ed and two males who were obviously having sex with the girl and have them remain in the room. Ed, the fraternity president, has by this time recognized you. The girl starts to cry quietly, the two males become very nervous, and the rest of the observers quickly vanish from the room.

"Bill," begins the president, extending his hand to you, "We were just having some harmless fun."

"I'm not so sure about that, Ed," you reply, pulling out a notepad and pen and ignoring his extended hand. You direct Ed to take the two males to an adjoining room and wait for you there. You turn back to the girl, who has by now managed in some fashion to get dressed. You ask her what was going on. All she can manage between quiet sobs is that she is scared and that her name is Yvonne. You try to encourage her that everything will be all right and ask her to remain in the room while you question Ed and the other two males next door. As you leave the room, you look up and see Dr. Madge Mullins, Assistant Dean of Students, walking toward you. You know her from your days as a student.

"Bill, I got a call from a student downstairs who works in my office. What's going on here?"

You quickly explain the situation to her as you know it. You can tell from the look on her face that she is both concerned and agitated.

"Bill, you said the girl's name was Yvonne? I've dealt with her before. She doesn't have the best reputation on campus. This is a university matter and I will guarantee you that this situation will be handled in an appropriate manner. There is no need for us to further embarrass this girl or the university, for that matter. You know what happens when these things get in the paper."

You carefully consider what Dean Mullins is saying. You also remember your sergeant's parting words. Do you let her take care of the situation or do you call Sergeant Womack?

Based on what you have read, answer the following questions:

1. Is this situation a university or police matter? Why? Does the fact that the young girl seems to have a "reputation" make a difference?

2. Are you subject to any liability issues in this case?

3. What do you feel would be a responsible and just outcome to this case? What additional information would you need in order to make an accurate assessment?

CASE 2
HOT DOG

You are a veteran police officer with twelve years of experience. You hold the rank of sergeant in the patrol division. Your lieutenant has asked you to help "break in" a rookie police officer who has just graduated from the police academy.

Your new partner's name is Eddie. Eddie is 22 years old and tells you he has a Bachelor's degree in Criminal Justice. You always wanted to get a degree in law enforcement or criminal justice but you have a son in college, which puts quite a strain on your family budget. Eddie tries to impress you with his education by referring to studies and theoretical aspects of modern law enforcement during the shift. You take Eddie's remarks in stride and tell him that knowing law enforcement is one thing and performing it is another.

During the first week you notice that on several calls, Eddie has acted harshly with people. He has also taken his nightstick out, slapped it in his hand, and toyed with it while talking to people. You mention it to him and he does not seem to listen. On one occasion, in a semi-serious way, Eddie threatened a restaurant waitress with a parking citation if she did not give him a police discount on his lunch. Eddie explained to you that he was only kidding the waitress. You try to explain that sometimes people take "kidding" the wrong way.

Eddie is always wanting you to stop vehicles on the highway for speeding. You tell Eddie that police officers cannot arrest everyone for exceeding the speed limit or everyone would be in jail. You allowed Eddie to handle one speeder on his own in order for him to learn the procedure. While you were sitting in your cruiser, it became obvious that Eddie and the speeder were shouting at each other. You got out of the cruiser and had to tell Eddie to get back to the cruiser and sit down before the situation deteriorated even further. The speeder had his children in the car and appeared to be angry. The speeder told you that Eddie chewed him out in front of his children and even used profanity. You apologized to the speeder and issued him a warning ticket. When you got back to your cruiser, Eddie was very angry. He told you that you should

13

have let him write the speeder up, as much for his disrespect as for his speeding. You tried to explain to Eddie that police officers must earn respect and not demand it from the public. You also explained that an officer must always try to treat the public with respect if he expects respect from the public. Eddie did not seem to listen.

Eddie is off today, and you are thankful you only have to ride with him a couple of days a week. The lieutenant calls you in to talk about Eddie. He asks you to go over to Eddie's house and talk with him. The lieutenant explains that there have been several complaints from Eddie's neighborhood about his behavior. It appears that Eddie has been "playing policeman" around the neighborhood while he has been off duty. As your cruiser comes to a stop in front of Eddie's house, you take a deep breath as you try to find the right words to say to Eddie.

Based on what you have read, answer the following questions:

1. Do you think Eddie is typical of most rookie police officers?
2. Do you think Eddie will "outgrow" his attitudes and manners?
3. Would you, as the sergeant, report Eddie's conduct during the speeding incident to the lieutenant and recommend that Eddie be terminated?
4. What should you say to Eddie now?

CASE 3
PARK PLACE

"Jimmy, if I catch you speeding one more time, I'm going to call your Daddy, and you know what that will mean," Officer Smith says as he hands the young man his third warning ticket in the last three months. "Doing sixty miles an hour in a school zone is unacceptable!"

"Yes Sir, Officer Smith. I promise I'll be more careful in the future," Jimmy replies. Jimmy's girlfriend, Lola, lights a cigarette and the two teenagers drive away to the sound of heavy metal music blaring from the car stereo.

Sergeant Bill Smith, your new partner, returns to the cruiser, stashes his clipboard, and turns on the ignition.

"You ready for a coffee break? They've got great latte down at the Croissant and Thistle coffee shop."

"Sure," you reply.

You order a hot chocolate while Bill asks for a croissant and latte. Once you get your drinks and food, Bill steers you to a quiet table in the corner.

"How's your hot chocolate?" Bill inquires. "Fine," you answer.

Swallowing the last of his croissant, your new partner clears his throat. "Jack, I know Park Place must seem like a different world from the South-side precinct, and I guess in a way it is. We do things differently here. Most of the folks are well-connected professionals—doctors and such. You might say our role is more supervision and less enforcement, like the young man I just pulled over for speeding. Jimmy Hamm's father is Reverend Dennis Hamm, Senior Pastor of a large, influential Baptist church. In fact, the mayor, a state senator, and four of the city commissioners attend his church. Jimmy's not a bad kid, just spoiled—although next time I catch him speeding, I *will* call his father. He knows if I talk to his father, I'll tell him about that white trash he's dating. And he knows that won't sit none too well with his father. If you have any questions, feel free to put 'em on the table."

"Well Sergeant," you begin, "this precinct is a lot different than the one I came from. In Southside, Jimmy would have gotten a ticket the first time we caught him. I know it's a lower income area, but I thought 'the law is the law'."

"It is. It is, Jack," Bill says with a chuckle. "The law is the law. It's just that we apply it differently here than you did in Southside. You'll be fine. I'll bet they didn't have hot chocolate made with real chocolate down in Southside."

As you walk to your car after the shift is over, you reflect on your first day in Park Place. It was definitely easier duty than where you had come from. Still, the knot in your gut lets you know you are uneasy about your new partner's approach to law enforcement.

Based on what you have read, answer the following questions:

1. Why is Jack troubled? Why isn't his partner, Bill, concerned?

2. Do more prominent neighborhoods expect special consideration from police departments and other government institutions? If so, why?

3. What are some possible negative consequences that could result from Sergeant Smith letting Jimmy off with another warning?

CASE 4
LIBERTY AND JUSTICE FOR ALL

You are a police officer in a large metropolitan city. For the past eight months you worked in a middle- and upper-class suburban patrol zone. Most of the people with whom you came in contact were respectable members of the community. You had good rapport with most of the community and they were generally quite cooperative with the police. Now you are being transferred to another patrol zone that is in a lower-class area near the inner city.

The first week you are in the new zone, you are assigned to work with Mike, a veteran officer who has been working this zone for almost four years. Mike drives you around, pointing out informants, drunks, thieves, and places where they hang out. You immediately notice that Mike has a somewhat harsh, even punitive attitude regarding the people with whom he comes in contact on his beat.

"You have to treat these people tough, intimidation is the only way to communicate with them," Mike explains.

After one week in your new zone, you become aware of a great difference in police work with different types of people. You rarely made arrests in your old zone. Most problems there could be worked out by talking rationally with the people with whom you came in contact. In this zone, however, you have made more arrests and have had to use more force with people. It becomes apparent to you that there are even more drunks and criminals living in the new zone than you had ever expected. People living in the slums seem to be more apathetic as well.

Mike has told you that if you need information on criminal activity, just pick somebody up and threaten to arrest them if they do not tell you what you need to know. This method worked, as your new partner seemed to demonstrate frequently. Mike would "plant" drugs or a gun on somebody, then threaten to arrest them if they did not give him information or become an informant for him. Mike has occasionally beat confessions out of suspects, then threatened to "get them" if they did not plead guilty to offenses.

You become aware of more violent crimes in your new zone. There are more murders, assaults, and rapes here than would happen in the middle- and upper-class neighborhoods. Mike defines rape "victims" as those persons who did not get paid for their services. "Not even worth writing a report on," Mike tells you. Murder investigations are routinely handled by the investigators in this zone. The detectives seldom perform a comprehensive investigation on any offense here. In the middle- and upper-class zone, all offenses were investigated thoroughly and the victims were given excellent attention by investigating officers.

You find that more police officers are assaulted in the lower-class zone than in your old zone. The people living in the lower-class zone do not appear to respect the police. It seems they only respect force.

"Don't ever turn your back on these people. And if you have to put one of these thugs down, be sure there ain't no damned video cameras around," Mike advises you. Mike also advises you to have your gun ready at all times.

"Shotgun's the best, they're really scared of 'em," says Mike. You also notice that more officers in this zone use deadly force than officers in other zones of the city. The police shot five people here last year.

"And probably a few more they didn't count," Mike chuckles.

After working in the new zone for two months and seeing what kind of people live in the area, you find yourself agreeing more and more with Mike's attitude and methods.

You and Mike receive a radio call to back up another unit a couple of blocks away. As you pull up beside the other cruiser, you see two police officers beating up a young man in the alley.

"C'mon Mike, you want a piece of this?" shouts one of the officers.

Mike takes out his slapjack and moves in with the other two officers beating the youth.

"What did he do?" you ask.

"He made the mistake of calling us names," responds one of the officers. "We're going to let this one be an example."

The young man could not be over seventeen years old and appears to be badly hurt. You know the officers will leave him in the alley when they are finished beating him. Of course, there will be no arrest.

You begin to think about how you have changed. Mike always says, "Fight fire with fire." Right now you are wondering who the criminals are. What should you do?

Based on what you have read, answer the following questions:

1. How would Mike respond to the community if the situation were reversed (i.e., if Mike were transferred to a higher-income neighborhood zone)?

2. What would happen if you, as the new officer in the zone, reported the incidents to your superiors?

3. How do police affect community relations in inner-city areas? What can the police do to help promote police-community relations in lower socioeconomic neighborhoods?

CASE 5
NO ESPAÑOL

You are a rookie police officer with only three months' experience. You are working the 4 P.M. to 12 A.M. shift in the northern section of Port Clarion, an area known for its high crime rate and large Cuban national population. You were assigned the northern section partly because all new rookie officers get the high-crime areas and partly because you could speak a little Spanish from courses you had in college.

Sergeant Pat West, a 29-year vet with the Port Clarion Police Department, has always gone out of his way to help you get acquainted with police work. Sergeant West was your training officer for six weeks. He's always talking about having one year left before retirement and about moving up north to be near his son and grandchildren. Sergeant West is one of those old-school cops that has only a high school education and can't speak anything but common (or uncommon) English. You notice that he is always a little uncomfortable when dealing with people of other cultures. Sergeant West, who normally works the beach area, is filling in for Sergeant Jackson of your shift, who is taking sick leave. You are looking forward to working with Sergeant West again tonight.

The majority of your shift has been fairly routine. However, about 10 P.M., you hear Sergeant West advising headquarters that he is stopping a car for suspected DUI. From the car's description, it sounds like Demingo Chavez's Lincoln Towncar. Chavez is a known drug dealer in the northern section. A few minutes later, you hear Sergeant West yelling on the radio that he needs assistance. You are only six blocks away, and it takes only a few minutes to reach Sergeant West's location.

Upon arriving, you observe Sergeant West hovering over two badly beaten Cuban men. West is holding his baton over his head, threatening to strike the injured men again. You get out of your cruiser and help West put the men into the back seat of his cruiser. Somewhat confused, you ask the sergeant what happened before you arrived.

"Damn Cubans . . . don't speak any English," West replied nervously. "I told them to stop but they just kept coming towards me, speaking some

19

kind of Cuban gibberish. They both made some sudden movements and I nailed the bastards."

You try to communicate with the men and discover that Demingo's younger brother, Fernando, was the driver of the car and his friend Sinco Santiago was the passenger. The moment Sergeant West pulled behind their car, Fernando began searching under the seats to make sure his brother had not left any drugs or other paraphernalia underneath the car seat.

"That's why I was swerving!" Fernando exclaims, holding his bleeding head.

Sergeant West explains that he had instructed the men to exit the vehicle and told them to place their hands in plain view. The men did not obey his orders and began fumbling in their pockets, speaking Spanish and coming toward him. Sergeant West took their actions as aggressive moves and felt threatened. West used his baton to sweep their legs from underneath them, but they were still making what West interpreted to be threatening moves. West said he had no choice but to respond more severely.

"I really appreciate your getting here so quickly, Corky. I don't believe I could have handled these guys without your help," Sergeant West explains.

The sergeant obviously made an error in judgment. The two men had not been making any aggressive moves—they simply did not understand what Sergeant West wanted them to do. The amount of force Sergeant West used on the two men will require them to have medical attention. It could have been avoided had Sergeant West been able to understand and speak a little Spanish. On the other hand, it also could have been avoided had the two men been able to understand English.

Based on what you have read, answer the following questions:

1. Should you report Sergeant West to superiors for excessive use of force? Why or why not?

2. What would you tell an internal affairs investigator if questioned about the incident?

3. Is Sergeant West responsible for the incident, either criminally or civilly? Who is to blame for the incident? How can such incidents be avoided in the future?

4. Do communities with cultural traditions and languages different from the dominant culture have a responsibility to learn how to communicate with law enforcement officers and other government officials?

CASE 6
COMMUNITY POLICING
NETWORK OR NIGHTMARE?

You have just been promoted to lieutenant in an East Coast police department that employs 450 officers. You rose quickly through the ranks in the last eight years, having started as a patrol officer in the historical district of the city. You were one of the first foot-and-bicycle officers in that district under the new community policing approach the department began six years ago. Because of your experience with community policing and your recent promotion to a mid-level supervisory position, you are now being transferred to another area of the city. This area, Greenberg community, is northwest of the historical district and is mainly composed of lower-class residential, single-family homes and a large public housing complex. There are a few small grocery stores, specialty shops, liquor stores, and repair shops within the community. You are replacing Lt. Vernon Sparks, who commanded the Greenberg Community Police Center for the past two years. Lt. Sparks, who was near retirement, requested a transfer to the historical district after experiencing some problems with the Greenberg Community Police program. He was granted the transfer by the chief of police.

"Well, Bill, congratulations on that promotion. You sure moved up fast in this department. It took me a full eighteen years to make lieutenant. Of course, that's how things are done now, you being a black fellow and all," Sparks states with a grin as he greets you at the Greenberg Community Police Center.

His prejudiced remarks do not really bother you that much. After all, you have seen much worse during your eight years as a police officer. Sparks worked his way up in the department the old fashioned way, with help from political friends and a lot of luck. The fact that you graduated at the top of your academy class, had two awards of valor from the city, and completed a master's degree in criminal justice did not seem to matter much to Sparks. He figured you were just one of the "token minorities" that got promoted.

21

"Well, Bill, let me fill you in on some of the problems here and turn you loose. I'm ready for a cushy job down in the historical district. Nothing to worry about down there but tourists and traffic. Anyway, as you know, we have 26 officers assigned to the Greenberg Center, open 24 hours a day, 7 days a week. Officers are encouraged to walk foot patrol or ride bicycles in nice weather, but they do have cruisers for bad weather and prisoner transport. Good luck getting them out of the cars, though. Very few will walk foot or ride them damn bicycles. They say the bicycles make 'em look like a bunch of girl scouts. Can't say as I disagree with them on that one," Lt. Sparks concludes with a chuckle.

The lieutenant's words about officers not wanting to walk foot patrols or ride bicycles do not surprise you. You are familiar with the problems of the Greenberg community. The community has not changed much in the past thirty years since you grew up there. Neither Sparks nor many others in the department know that you were raised by a single mother living just two blocks from what is now the Police Center.

"You know, Bill, last year we had to put Plexiglas in that front window just because it was broken out so many times by the young hoodlums here. Officers don't ride bicycles because they get shot at with pellet guns, and people laugh at them in those shorty pants and stuff. I dunno what the chief thinks about this community police thing, but it ain't proper police work. They expect us to coddle these people and not enforce the law. We need to get back on the streets in cars in order to properly ride herd on crime in these areas. Well, I guess you'll find out soon enough once you've been here awhile," Sparks advises.

It is easy to understand why officers are not encouraged to walk beats or ride bicycles with the outgoing commander's attitude and opinion about police work being what it is.

Two days later you overhear your desk officer giving advice to an elderly lady who walked into the Police Center. "Look lady, I don't know about your social security stuff. You need to talk with the welfare office downtown."

"Well, I don't have a phone, could I use yours?" the lady asks meekly.

"No, that's against policy. There's a pay phone over on that wall over there."

"Do you have their number?" the lady asks.

"There's a phone book with the phone over there, you can look it up. Now, excuse me, I have some paperwork to do," the officer states as he turns away from the lady to pick up some file folders on a desk.

"Officer Cupp, I couldn't help overhearing your conversation. Do you get many requests like that here?" you ask.

"Yes, Lt. Jackson, quite a few. Why, just the other day some joker comes in here and wants to know how he could get his power back on at his house. Like we were the power board or something. That's exactly what I told him too. I said, 'What the hell do I look like—an electrician?' Sent him on his way. Boy, some people . . ."

"Yes, Officer Cupp, I get the picture," you interrupt. "I have a better idea. Why don't you take this nice lady downtown to the Welfare Department. Take her to the appropriate office. Introduce her to the appropriate social worker. Stay with her until she gets her problem straightened out. And bring her back and drop her off at her residence. Then, report back to me here."

"I beg your pardon, Lieutenant?" Cupp asks with a confused and befuddled look clouding his face.

"You heard me, Officer Cupp. I'll watch the desk while you're gone," you state.

"Yessir, Lieutenant, but I believe it's against policy to . . ."

"I make the policy here, Officer Cupp," you interrupt, no longer smiling.

Turning to the elderly woman, you continue: "Ma'am, this officer is going to take you down to the welfare office and see that you get to talk with the appropriate person about your social security, OK?"

"Oh, thank you and God bless you, young man."

A few months have now passed since you took over the Greenberg Community Police Center. You are called downtown to the chief's office to report on your first three months at the center. After the traditional small talk, you begin: "Chief, I do have a few problems I'd like to discuss with you. Mainly it's about a network system with other agencies. We get complaints about all sorts of community problems: welfare, public utilities, even when garbage is supposed to be picked up. We have to refer these people to the appropriate agency, but most of them are downtown here and most of our community residents have no reliable transportation, phone, or much money for bus fares and so on. I was wondering if we could . . ."

"Yes, Lt. Jackson," interrupts the chief. "I've heard about your problems. I've heard that you're running taxi service over there with police vehicles. Why, I even heard that one of your officers had to do some electrical work at somebody's house?"

"It was just a blown fuse at this old lady's house," you respond. "The officer just screwed in a new one. The lady couldn't afford an electrician to come out and it was just a single . . ."

"Yes, I see," interrupts the chief again. "Well, we're police officers, not social workers, Bill. We don't have the resources to do everything for these people. Now I know you have a special place in your heart for them, but you've got to get things in perspective. Do police work, Bill, the rest will take care of itself," the chief advises, pouring himself another cup of coffee.

You leave the chief's office disappointed and feeling, for the first time in your career, like a failure. You thought you were doing the right thing in helping the community with their nonpolice problems. You feel the chief has it backwards. If you could help the community with their problems, the police work would take care of itself. After all, in only three short months you have noticed a change in community attitudes about the police. More people are coming to the center, not only to ask for help on nonpolice matters, but also to report on drug activities, thefts, burglaries, and other crime problems. Some of the citizens on the volunteer auxiliary nightwatch are even trying to help the police catch the bad guys. Even your officers have started to experience a greater enjoyment in their work with the community.

After mulling over your disappointment for several days, you decide to ask to meet with the chief again. However, you will need to be prepared next time for his narrow perspective. What are you going to do and say? How are you going to get through to him? Is there another way to provide the people with the help that they need? What is the proper balance between police work and social and community services?

Based on what you have read, answer the following questions:

1. What is the community policing philosophy? What is it supposed to do for police and community relations?

2. Should the police be involved in nonpolice activities? How much time do officers usually spend on nonpolice work? Should they be fighting crime rather than being social workers?

3. How would you react to the chief's statements? What would you do and say that would support your position?

CASE 7
OFFICER FRIENDLY—
UNFRIENDLY NEIGHBORHOOD

You are a police-community relations officer in a police department serving a city of 250,000 people. Your primary duties are concerned with community crime prevention programs and providing educational seminars to schools and civic groups. You enjoy your job and feel you are making a contribution in the efforts to decrease criminal activity in your city. Just last year your seven-person Police Community Relations (PCR) unit was cited by the mayor as being largely responsible for the continuing decrease in burglaries in your city over the past three years. The mayor's recognition also resulted in a positive special feature article in the local newspaper, complete with a picture of you and your unit.

The PCR unit was your first assignment after graduating from the academy five years ago. Since then, you have helped organize numerous neighborhood watch programs, a fleet watch program with telephone and utility workers, a police scout program with teenagers, and an operation identification program.

While you are preparing for tomorrow's speaking engagement at a junior high school on a "DARE" anti-drug program, your sergeant enters your office.

"Jim, sorry to interrupt you, but I need to speak with you for a moment."

"Sure, Sarge, let me find a place for you to sit down," you state, clearing away some pamphlets from a chair.

"Jim, as you know, Officer Adams' wife is ready to have her baby at any time now, so I'm trying to keep his schedule as flexible as I can in case he has to go to the hospital."

"I know. Adams has been a nervous wreck all week," you respond with a grin.

The sergeant continues, "Adams is scheduled for a neighborhood watch meeting tonight at the Pinecrest community, and I'd like to have you go instead. I'll give you some time off today to compensate."

"Sure thing, I'll be glad to help. After all, Adams helped me the time I had those night classes at the university," you state.

"Good," replies the sergeant. "Let me fill you in on Pinecrest community. As you know, it's an older neighborhood, mainly retired and senior citizens, lower middle-class, blue-collar families. Criminal Investigation has informed us that burglaries and larcenies are on an increase there. Also, there's been some increase in violent crime, muggings, assaults and so on. Seems like some of the younger thugs have moved over there for some easy targets. We've gotten several complaints from the residents on gang activity and crime. A lot of those people are angry."

"I take it that this is the community's first neighborhood watch meeting?" you ask.

"Yes. Adams set it up a couple of days ago with John Webster, the pastor at the church there on the corner of Oak and Dale. Webster scheduled a meeting with the residents at his church tonight at 7."

"I'll go through the usual routine on starting a watch program tonight and then try to set up monthly meetings with them," you respond.

"OK, Jim. Thanks a lot," replies your sergeant, leaving your office.

There never seem to be enough hours in the day. After hurrying through supper at a local fast-food restaurant, you arrive for the meeting a few minutes late. As you hand out pamphlets to the residents in the meeting hall at the church, you notice that most of the people seem apprehensive and, in some cases, unfriendly.

"Probably the uniform," you think to yourself.

You walk to the podium and begin: "Ladies and gentlemen, may I have your attention. I'm certainly glad you were able to make it here tonight for our first neighborhood watch meeting. I'm Officer Jim Mabry. You should all have some pamphlets that I passed around. We can go over these later after the videotape presentation," you state while preparing the videotape machine.

"Officer Mabry," says one of the citizens, raising his hand near the back of the room.

"Uh, yes sir, we'll have time for questions and discussions after the videotape," you interrupt.

"Well, all I wanted to know is what are you boys doing about the crime problem in Pinecrest?" states the man anyway, with several of the people around him voicing their support for his question.

"That's what I'm here for . . ." you respond.

Looking around and gaining confidence, the man continues, "Look, I haven't seen as many as one cop do a damn thing around here. Why don't you boys go out here and arrest these hoodlums? You all make it sound as if it's our fault we're being robbed and mugged. I know several of my neighbors who didn't come here tonight 'cause they were afraid to go out after dark. We don't need no slide shows and pamphlets—we need action." Several of the citizens angrily shout their support for his words.

"Young man, young man. . . ." A frail-looking older woman in the front row tries to get your attention by waving her pamphlets at you.

"Yes ma'am?" you respond.

"Are you a real policeman?" she asks.

Based on what you have read, answer the following questions:

1. How should you respond to the crowd? Can you gain their respect and adequately address the problems they have with crime in their community?

2. What resources could you use to help you deal with the angry residents?

3. What are some advantages and disadvantages in establishing neighborhood watch programs and police-community relations approaches in general?

CASE 8
HATE CRIMES

Being a state trooper is all you ever wanted to do since you took your first criminal justice course at the local community college. Uncle Tom, a deputy in the sheriff's department for over 20 years, has also been a positive influence in your lifelong ambition to work in law enforcement. A happy marriage, a new baby, and a new career as a state trooper—as far as you are concerned, it can't get any better than this.

You are assigned to the graveyard shift in a large rural county, one of the special assignments given to the new troopers. You occasionally see a sheriff's patrol car, but usually not after midnight. For the most part, you are on your own. At 2:30 A.M. you receive a call from the dispatcher regarding a car wreck on Highway 27.

Arriving at the scene of the accident, you observe a late model station wagon in the ditch next to the highway, its headlights shining into the woods. A county emergency services vehicle is already there applying first aid to a hysterical white female who appears to be in her mid-twenties. An older male is standing next to a pickup truck. It turns out that he was the person who drove by, saw the accident, and went for help. The paramedics are having an animated conversation with a black male who appears to be in his early thirties. You get out of your cruiser and walk toward the medics.

A medic pulls you off to the side. "Trooper Stevens, this man needs to be taken to Upton County Hospital, but he refuses to go. We've done all we can for him here. See if you can talk some sense into him."

You ask the medics to let you talk to him privately. Turning to the injured man, you notice not only that he has cuts (apparently from his head making contact with the car's windshield) but that his face is puffy, his nose broken, and the way he is cradling his left arm suggests that it is also injured, possibly broken. After introducing yourself, you reassure him that you are there to help and that he needs to go to the hospital. After considerable coaxing, the man, whose name is Ned, tells you why he won't go.

"My wife and I stopped for a sandwich at a diner about ten miles back. When we pulled back on to the road, minding our own business, two truckloads of fools who followed us out of the parking lot ran us off into that ditch. When I came to, they were beating the hell out of me, calling me a nigger and my wife a whore!" At this point, Ned starts crying. "Who do they think they are! I though they were going to kill her and me. They told me they weren't gonna let any niggers and their white whores live in Upton county. I got a good job and I work hard, but it ain't worth my life."

"What did the men look like? Did you hear anyone mention any names?" you ask as you take notes. What Ned says next makes you feel a huge knot forming in your stomach.

"I couldn't see none of the faces. They all wore camouflage ski masks. One of them did say not to bother reporting any of this to the sheriff's department and then they all laughed. And one of them said to the others that if I did, I would have to answer to Tom."

After conferring with the medics, you call ahead and arrange to have Ned and his wife taken to a neighboring county hospital. Thanking the farmer for stopping and helping, you return to your cruiser. You sit there a long time staring out into the night. You have always known that Uncle Tom as well as several of your other relatives are prejudiced, but they are from another generation. You don't agree with them, but they are basically good people who work hard, go to church, and raise their families as best they can. You find it hard to believe that any of them would participate in anything like this. There is a hate crimes unit with the state bureau of investigation. You could contact them or . . . ?

Based on what you have read, answer the following questions:

1. Can people who are prejudiced be good citizens in other areas of their lives?

2. You are torn by loyalty to your uncle and your role as a law enforcement officer. How should you resolve this conflict?

3. How is this issue a community as well as a law enforcement issue?

Section II

FAMILY AND CRISIS INTERVENTION

Introduction

A major part of the police service role deals with a variety of interpersonal crises. Quarreling family members, street disturbances, neighborhood disputes, landlord-tenant disputes, child abuse, alcoholism, drug-related incidents, and mental disorders are but a few of the crises with which a police officer is faced. The primary objective of the police regarding crisis intervention calls is to restore and preserve the peace and safety of individuals involved in the disturbance, as well as to the community. Crisis intervention calls represent the most frequent requests for police services. Although many of these calls are related to criminal offenses, some are of a civil nature and not within the area of police jurisdiction.

The average citizen exhibits little knowledge regarding the limits of police authority. His or her only concern is that a grievance or dispute must be settled. In their anger or frustration, citizens turn often to the police for assistance. Even though the source of the citizen's concern may be of a civil nature, the police have the responsibility to restore order and preserve the peace. The manner in which this task is undertaken may be instrumental in the prevention of a civil matter from becoming a criminal one.

The lethal nature of police crisis intervention is grimly registered in police statistics. Over 20 percent of the total number of police officers killed in the line of duty meet their deaths while intervening in such crisis

31

situations as family fights and street disturbance calls (U.S. Department of Justice, 2001). Whenever a police officer responds to a crisis intervention call he or she must be prepared for anything. A lax attitude in responding to a call may contribute to the seriousness of the circumstances. In order to perform his or her responsibility effectively, the police officer must maintain constant vigilance, critically survey and analyze the situation, use interpersonal communication and anticipate the unexpected (Hirschel, Dean, and Lumb, 1994).

Family Disputes

There are few assignments considered more distasteful to a police officer than a family dispute. In these tension-packed moments, emotions are inclined to escalate. The individuals involved may say and do things from which they would normally refrain. In many cases, family members redirect their anger toward the intervening police officer.

In comparison to middle- and upper-class individuals, persons from lower-class neighborhoods are more likely to call the police during family disputes. While the reasons might vary, they seem to include: (1) the prohibitive expense of professional helping services; (2) lack of awareness of free or inexpensive community mental health services; (3) perceived stigma of going to a professional mental health practitioner; (4) familiarity with police presence and intervention in such matters; (5) severity and frequency of the abuse; (6) presence of dependent children; and (7) the abuser's use of alcohol (Roberts, 1997). The opposite seems true concerning persons from upper and middle classes involved in family disputes. They seem more likely to utilize alternative professional helping services rather than call the police.

The police officer, upon entering a home involved in a family dispute, should remember that not all family disputes involve the commission of a crime. Police officers should be aware that families who have requested police services are in need of outside intervention for problems that may have progressed beyond the point of self-mediation or control. Therefore, it is important that the officer avoid creating an impression of disinterest, cynicism, or belittlement of the problems for which the officer has been summoned.

When intervening in a dispute of a violent nature involving physical contact, immediate police action must be initiated. Physical intervention on the part of the police officers may be necessary in this type of disturbance. Officers responding to such calls should place themselves in a position that will limit the possibility of personal injury. The intervening officers should separate the persons involved and make a wide visual survey of the area for objects that could be used as weapons. Once this has been accomplished, the officers may assess the situation further to determine if formal police action is in order.

It is very common for alcohol to be involved in family disputes. It is difficult to gather the facts accurately in a dispute if one of the persons involved has been drinking. Some intoxicated persons are violent in disputes. Intervening police officers should remain professionally objective when dealing with an intoxicated individual and indicate that they want to help, but should not demonstrate too much sympathy for his or her intoxicated condition.

When intervening in any family dispute, the police should utilize tact, sensitivity, and interpersonal communication skills. There has been substantial documentation regarding the need for police officers to possess and demonstrate such skills in domestic crisis situations (Braswell and Meeks, 1982; Hirschel, Hutchison, and Dean, 1999). These findings are of particular significance for interpersonal intervention, given the amount of time an officer spends answering such calls and the number of officers injured or killed while attempting to resolve such problem situations (U.S. Department of Justice, 2001).

Neubauer (1974), in his study of a midwestern city of 900,000, reported the attitudes of the local police toward family disputes. Police officers had little training on which to rely, short of common sense. Police powers of arrest were limited on private property. The complainant (usually the wife) often was hesitant to file charges but wanted the police to do something to quiet the husband. If the police did make an arrest, the other spouse frequently became belligerent with the officers. Generally, police officers saw little point in making arrests on such calls anyway since it would . . . "probably end up taking the food money for the kids to pay the fine" (Neubauer, 1974). Breci's (1989) study of Midwest and southeast police officers tended to support Neubauer's findings.

If family dispute calls are being processed by officers who are untrained or unsure of their abilities to manage the crisis intervention successfully, two things are likely to occur and in fact frequently do occur. Either the police are viewed as incompetent professionals or as heavy-handed intruders in a private situation (Breci, 1989; Hirschel, Hutchison, and Dean, 1999). However, with careful training, motivation, and aptitude on the part of police officers, such views of the police can be avoided and police injuries can be decreased.

Reiser (1973), Aguilera (1990), and Gilliland (1993) have suggested a three-phase approach to police intervention in family disputes. The first phase is the initial intervention; the second consists of a combination of defusing and assessment; and, the third phase involves resolution and/or referral. The initial intervention is the most critical phase and involves six ground rules: (1) stay calm, (2) do not threaten, (3) do not take sides, (4) do not challenge a man's masculinity, (5) do not degrade a woman's femininity, and (6) give verbal escape routes to help people save face. The defusing and assessment phase involves listening to all involved parties without taking sides. The listening approach allows individuals to "blow off steam" and release the tension and hostility. This "defuses" a potentially explosive situation as well as allows the intervening police officer the opportunity to assess the situation. The officer may be able to determine through tactful questioning the frequency of the family disputes, how long the disputes have existed, what caused the disputes, and what the underlying motives are for the disputes. The police officer may find that one or more of the parties have emotional problems that require professional help. The third phase, resolution and/or referral, requires the intervening police officer to make a judgment about the situation. The officer may allow the disputing parties to help make this judgment. If their response seems realistic and agreeable, the dispute can be resolved at that point. However, if desirable and/or necessary, a referral to a helping agency should be made.

One of the standard procedures that has been developed for police intervention in family disputes involves having two officers respond to the call together and separating the disputing parties, with one officer going with each person into a separate room. The officer then allows the person to talk and explain the situation, asking questions for the purpose of clarification. The officers then switch with each other to check out the stories and obtain a better evaluation of the total situation. The couple is then brought together to tell their side to each other, but allowing only one person to talk at a time. The police officers are then able to point out discrepancies, contradictions, or common feelings, and obtain a reaction from the disputing parties after making suggestions.

Crisis Intervention

Farmer and Kowalewski (1976) use two terms to illustrate the police officer's role in dealing with crises: crisis intervention and crisis management. Crisis management is defined as "the police response to situations when officers act primarily as law officers rather than as helping agents." The police officers attempt to contain community conflict or prevent police contact with an individual from developing into an uncontrollable situation. Such attempts keep the peace in the community, uphold the law, and minimize the use of force. While arrests may be necessary, they are undertaken as a last, not first, resort. Police objectives should be to identify the cause of the crisis, to assist the individual in meeting the impact of the crisis, and to mobilize appropriate helping agency resources. The main objective for police officers intervening in a crisis situation is to bring the case to a close as a police matter while securing the necessary help for those involved.

There are four roles that third-party intervenors play in crisis situations: (1) the advocate, (2) the conciliator, (3) the mediator, and (4) the arbitrator (Hendricks and Byers, 1996). The advocate represents a person or a group entering a crisis conflict situation as an advisor or consultant to one of the disputing groups. The advocate is not neutral in the conflict. He or she contributes skills as an organizer to one of the disputing groups, helping to create a structure capable of taking action and advising the group on the formulation of demands and on sources of support. In some situations the advocate in a dispute may be seen as an outside agitator, particularly when his or her function is to escalate a conflict in order to bring the issues to a head and to achieve change. As a result of the late 1960s riots, attitudes toward advocates in community conflicts have changed. It is generally believed that the more highly organized and successfully led the protest group, the greater the opportunity to avoid irrationality and violence. Although the advocate contributes to conflict regulation, emotions continually escalate and are unpredictable, and the conflict may still mount to a crisis situation.

The conciliator attempts to cool down tempers by creating a physical and/or emotional distance between the conflicting groups and by making suggestions that may temporarily resolve the crisis conflict. The action of conciliators are distinguished from advocates because they represent the interests of both sides in a conflict (Hendricks and Byers, 1996).

Mediators have been defined as those third parties who are acceptable to all conflicting groups or persons in a dispute and help them in reaching a mutually satisfactory settlement of their differences (Hendricks and Byers, 1996). In distinguishing between conciliators and mediators, one might state that conciliators produce the environment in which mediation is possible. Sometimes mediators are also called negotiators, because they offer neutral meeting locations, interpret each side's position for the other, carry messages back and forth, and by using steady, optimistic attitudes facilitate a compromise and resolution of the conflict whenever possible.

Arbitrators are similar to mediators but have one additional function—to make a judgment for one party or all conflicting parties in order to settle the dispute. Police officers intervening in a crisis conflict are usually seen as arbitrators. Arbitrators, like mediators, must be acceptable to both sides in a conflict before making any arbitrary judgments. Police officers must often first play all roles in a conflict before being acceptable as an arbitrator.

Police officers intervening in a crisis conflict must play the role of advocate, conciliator, mediator, and arbitrator. By separating and listening to each side, officers are able to play the role of advocate, opening lines of communication and enjoining respect from the conflicting parties. As conciliator, the police officer may be able to resolve a conflict situation temporarily by suggesting that one or both of the conflicting parties follow a course of action. As a mediator, the police officer may allow both conflicting parties to resolve their crisis on their own and work out their own problems without conflict. As an arbitrator, the police officer may resolve the situation on his or her own by taking an overt or other course of action. The role of arbitrator should be the last resort. The police officer, as an arbitrator in a crisis situation, is almost always blamed by one or both of the conflicting parties because of the officer's authority (Hendricks and Byers, 1996; Roberts, 1998).

Crisis Intervention Skills

Police officers should demonstrate an interest in acting in a helping role; they should possess emotional maturity in a sense that the officer can accept the responsibility for his or her actions and can live with the outcome of a crisis intervention. A nonjudgmental attitude is vital. It is important that the police officer be able to assess a crisis situation and face his or her client without imposing personal views and values. It is also essential that the police officer possess patience and a willingness to explore every possible avenue for solution to a problem before breaking off contact, making a referral, or using the power of arrest.

While one of the prime reasons for police officers to employ crisis intervention methods is to avoid arrest, the officer should not hesitate to use such authority when common sense indicates that a particular situation may not be resolved through the use of crisis intervention techniques.

The successful police crisis intervention officer must accept a dual role: that of being primarily a helping agent, but also one who must employ his or her enforcement authority when an occasion merits such a response (Braswell and Meeks, 1982).

Domestic Violence

During the early 1970s, police training in crisis intervention for domestic disturbances was inclined to stress a nonarrest approach. The police, often unsure of their legal authority in private homes, responded to domestic disturbances with a peacekeeping attitude. Some police departments even created crisis intervention units to relieve patrol officers of the burden of handling domestic disputes. The police response emphasis was on diverting family members away from the criminal justice system and into mental health, welfare, and other social service agencies. While such an emphasis is noble and directed at helping families, the police often became increasingly reluctant to utilize what police authority they did have in crisis intervention situations. Prosecuting attorneys also became more reluctant to press charges in family dispute cases.

It should be noted that there is a difference between domestic disturbances and domestic violence. Domestic disturbances may not involve physical injuries or threats of physical violence. In such disturbances, the police may be proper in acting primarily as a helping agent.

In the late 1970s and early 1980s, concerned feminists and other civil rights groups began to criticize the police for not adequately protecting women in domestic violence situations (Bae, 1981). When domestic disputes became violent, wives were usually the victims (Bell, 1984). Battered-spouse programs and emergency shelters further accentuated the concern regarding the police response to domestic violence.

A research project sponsored by the National Institute of Justice was conducted in Minneapolis to determine if police could decrease repeated spousal assault calls by treating offenders differently (Sherman and Berk, 1984). An experiment was designed to randomly test three strategies for police addressing domestic violence. The objective was to determine which of the three strategies—counseling the offender, separating the two parties, or formal arrest—would reduce future incidents of domestic violence.

The results of the Minneapolis study found that arresting offenders had the most impact on repeated calls for police service over a six-month period. Arresting and holding spousal assault offenders in jail appeared to reduce future incidents of domestic violence and was more effective than either counseling or sending the offender away (Sherman and Berk, 1984).

Since the results of studies, such as the Minneapolis experiment, have indicated the need for greater powers of arrest for police officers handling domestic violence cases, a large number of states have enacted new legislation toward that end (Sherman, 1986). Numerous states have enacted laws making spousal abuse a separate criminal offense, and many states have legislated probable cause arrest discretion for police even if they did not witness the misdemeanor assault in domestic violence situations. Some police departments have adopted policies requiring mandatory arrest of suspected offenders of spousal abuse. Sherman's (1986) survey found that an increasing proportion of police departments view arrest as the preferred method of dealing with spousal abuse offenders.

While arrest of domestic violence offenders appears to be most effective in the police response, some criticisms of the practice have surfaced (Gelles and Loseke, 1993; Hirschel, Hutchison, and Dean, 1999). It is generally known that victims of spousal abuse rarely wish to prosecute the offender. They simply want to be able to call the police to come and stop the abuse when necessary. Arresting the offender may create a more abusive situation for the victim later. The measure of effectiveness of arrest has been the number of "callbacks" to the same address. If a victim realizes that the abuser will most likely go to jail if the police are summoned, the victim may very well not call the police on future assaults. While this may appear to the police as a measure of successfully resolving the problem, the primary problem of domestic violence still has not been addressed and may now be a hidden statistic. Some current research has called for increased concern of police officials to this problem and even a return to more traditional counseling, mediation and crisis intervention methods in domestic violence cases (Breci and Simons, 1987; Breci, 1989; Yellott, 1990; Hirschel, Hutchison, and Dean, 1992; Gelles and Loseke, 1993).

Abuse of the Elderly

The abuse of elderly persons has increasingly become a topic of interest and concern in recent years. Elderly abuse is not generally reported to police as frequently as other crimes of assault and child abuse (Forst, 2000). Medical and human services workers are most likely to discover cases of elderly abuse and report these cases to the police. One reason for the nondiscovery of elderly abuse is the low visibility many elderly persons maintain. Unlike abused children who are more highly visible at schools or with friends, the elderly may stay indoors and venture out only occasionally.

Unlike child abuse and spousal abuse (in many states) where the police are sure of their legal standing in intervening, elderly abuse poses a legal problem for the police. Being adults, the elderly are not protected by child abuse statutes. The police generally have no legal right to intervene in misdemeanor assault of the elderly or negligence in elderly care if the victim does not wish to prosecute. In addition, spousal abuse and domestic violence laws in most states do not cover children's abuse of their parents. Therefore, the police may have to depend a great deal on the legal authority of social workers, mental health professionals and medical personnel in order to assist abused elderly persons effectively.

Other Crisis Incidents

It should also be noted that police officers need to be able to utilize effective crisis intervention skills in such areas as "barricaded subject incidents" where a person has a weapon, is in a state of psychological crisis, and is a threat to him- or herself or others. "High-risk suicide attempts" where a person threatens to use weapons or other forms of violence to endanger not only him- or herself, but also estranged family members or even onlookers are frequent calls for police service where effective crisis intervention skills are a necessity. "Mental health and other high-risk warrants" that involve police officers interacting with and apprehending emotionally disturbed persons and potentially dangerous felons, including drug dealers, are further examples of the need for effective police crisis intervention and interpersonal communication skills (McManis and Mullins, 1996).

Summary

Crisis intervention calls represent the most frequent requests for police services. Although crisis intervention includes a broad range of interpersonal crises such as child abuse, drug abuse, suicide, rape, and mental disorder, family dispute calls are the most typical and frequently the most dangerous for police officers. Police intervention in such disputes places the police officers in the dual role of enforcer and helping agent. While most police officers have had training as enforcement agents, few officers have the training or skill that adequately prepares them as helping agents in family disputes. The fact that there is little training for such skills emphasizes the concern of many police officers that acting as a social worker in family disputes is not a police duty. Many states have supported this view by enacting domestic violence legislation that increases the powers of the police intervening in such cases.

References

Aguilera, D. (1997). *Crisis Intervention: Theory & Methodology*, 8th ed. St. Louis: Mosby.

Bae, R. P. (1981). "Ineffective Crisis Intervention Techniques: The Case of the Police." *Crime and Justice*, 4:61–82.

Bell. D. J. (1984). "Police Response to Domestic Violence: An Exploratory Study." *Police Studies*, 7:23–30.

Braswell, M., and R. Meeks (1982). "The Police Officer as a Marriage and Family Therapist: A Discussion of Some Issues," *Family Therapy*, 9(12).

Breci, M. (1989). "The Effect of Training on Police Attitudes Toward Family Violence: Where Does Mandatory Arrest Fit In?" *Journal of Crime & Justice*, 12(1): 35–49.

Breci, M., and R. Simons (1987). "An Examination of Organizational and Individual Factors that Influence Police Response to Domestic Disturbances." *Journal of Police Science and Administration*, 15(2): 93–104.

Farmer, R. E., and V. A. Kowalewski (1976). *Law Enforcement and Community Relations*. Reston, VA: Reston Publishing Co.

Forst, C. S. (2000). *The Aging of America: A Handbook for Police Officers*. Springfield, IL: Charles C. Thomas.

Gelles, R., and D. Loseke. (1993). *Current Controversies on Family Violence*. Newburg Park, CA: Sage.

Gilliland, B. (1997). *Crisis Intervention Strategies*, 3d ed. Pacific Grove, CA: Brooks/Cole.

Hendricks, J. E., and B. Byers. (1996). *Crisis Intervention in Criminal Justice/Social Services*, 2d ed. Springfield, IL: Charles C. Thomas.

Hirschel, J. D., I. W. Hutchison, and C. W. Dean. (1999). "The Law Enforcement Response to Spouse Abuse." In L. Gaines and G. Cordner (eds.), *Policing Perspectives: An Anthology*. Lost Angeles: Roxbury Publishing Co.

McManis, M. S. and W. C. Mullins. (1996). *Crisis Negotiations*. Cincinnati: Anderson Publishing Co.

Neubauer, D. W. (1974). *Criminal Justice in Middle America*. Morristown, NJ: General Learning Press.

Reiser, M. (1973). *Practical Psychology for Police Officers*. Springfield, IL: Charles C Thomas.

Roberts, A. R. (1997). *Social Work in Juvenile and Criminal Justice Settings*, 2d ed. Springfield, IL: Charles C. Thomas.

———. (1998). *Battered Women and Their Families: Intervention Strategies and Treatment Programs*, 2d ed. New York: Springer Publishing Co.

Sherman, L. W. (1986). *Police Change Policy on Domestic Violence*. Washington, DC: Crime Control Institute.

Sherman, L. W., and R. A. Berk (1984). *The Minneapolis Domestic Violence Experiment*. Washington, DC: The Police Foundation.

————. (1984). "Specific Deterrent Effects of Arrest for Domestic Assault," *American Sociological Review*, 49 (April).

U.S. Department of Justice. (2001). *Law Enforcement Officers Killed and Assaulted*. Washington, DC: FBI Uniform Crime Reports.

Yellott, A. (1990). "Mediation and Domestic Violence: A Call for Collaboration," *Mediation Quarterly*, 8(1): 39–50.

CASES INVOLVING FAMILY AND CRISIS INTERVENTION

One of the more difficult duties of a police officer is the handling of complaints concerning family crises. The officer must enter into a situation of which he or she has little, if any, knowledge and preserve the peace. The manner in which the officer responds to these situations is the key to what can be a peaceful, even therapeutic, resolution of the problem or tragedy. It may be wise to keep in mind that more officers are assaulted while responding to family disturbance calls than for any other single category of police work.

Case number one, "Christmas Eve," examines the routine approach many officers utilize in answering family disturbance calls. Although family crisis intervention calls are commonplace in police work, they pose special problems during the holiday season that cannot be routinely handled.

Case number two, "Between a Rock and a Hard Place," is concerned with a dispute over child custody. Serving court orders can sometimes create dangerous and frustrating situations for an officer. In this case, a deputy sheriff must take custody of a small child and deliver the child to the rightful mother. The child's mother is obviously unfit in the eyes of the officer as well as the child's grandmother. Regardless of the right or wrong aspects of the situation, the officer feels he must carry out his duty.

Case number three, "Police Officer or Social Worker," attempts to portray a family crisis situation which the police may be unprepared to resolve. Police officers are frequently cast in the role of psychologist, counselor, or social worker when dealing with family problems regardless of whether or not they have received adequate training.

Case number four, "Different Choices, Equal Protection?" deals with the legal, as well as the emotional, task of handling a domestic violence situation involving homosexuals. Police officers find themselves in a situation where they must address their own fears, prejudices and legal standing in dealing with a homosexual couple involved in domestic violence.

Case number five, "Honor Thy Father and Mother," is concerned with the problem of elderly abuse. A police officer and a social services worker must decide how to deal with a son who abuses his elderly parents.

41

Case number six, "The Color of a Living Room," explores how a simple disagreement between a husband and wife can result in a serious encounter with the police. Two officers, a male and his female partner, answer a family disturbance call. The female officer finds that she must handle both her angered partner and the family in a delicate manner.

Case number seven, "Public Duty or Brotherhood," deals with a police officer who has received a family disturbance call at another police officer's home. Upon arriving, the officer finds a group of community members gathered outside the home waiting to see how the situation is handled. The officer realizes that he should perform his duty in order to maintain a working relationship with the community. The officer is also aware of the problems associated with arresting a fellow officer.

Case number eight, "Double Bind," points toward a temptation and problem to which police officers may be subjected—romantic and extramarital affairs that may interfere with their professional duties. In this case a police officer and his partner answer a domestic disturbance call. The officer recognizes the wife as being the girlfriend of his divorced partner.

CASE 1
CHRISTMAS EVE

You are a police officer responding to a family disturbance call. It is Christmas Eve and your department has a skeleton force working the 3 to 11 P.M. shift, so you are alone on the call.

You recognize the address of the complaint. You have been there previously on the same type of call. The house to which you are en route contains a man, his wife, and two young children. The husband, Charlie Adams, drinks heavily and subsequently becomes obnoxious. You assume that Charlie is drunk again. In the past, you have been able to calm Charlie down by threatening to take him to jail.

When you arrive at the scene, you notice an out-of-state car parked in the driveway and wonder if the Adamses have family in for the holidays. You advise the dispatcher that you have arrived and get out of your cruiser. While walking up to the front porch, you can hear loud arguing coming from inside the house.

After you have knocked on the door several times, Charlie opens it. He is obviously intoxicated and becomes agitated when he sees you. He asks what you want and you explain that you received a call from the neighbors again. You add that you are becoming tired of having to quiet him so frequently. Charlie's wife is behind him in the living room and angrily suggests that you lock him up.

There are other people in the living room and Charlie indicates they are his in-laws. As you step inside the living room you notice several bottles of liquor sitting on the table. Everyone apparently has been drinking. Using a familiar ploy, you tell Charlie that if he does not keep quiet you will take him to jail.

Mrs. Adams comes up to you and begins telling you that Charlie has become a nuisance and she wants him out of the house. The brother-in-law also begins to talk negatively about Charlie. Mrs. Adams continues her tirade by telling you that Charlie is an unfit father and hates the children.

The two children come into the living room to see what is happening. Mrs. Adams tells the children to go to their room because Daddy is drunk again.

Suddenly, Charlie screams at his wife and, grabbing her by the hair, begins to slap her. The two guests retreat in fear to the other end of the room. You quickly attempt to separate the two, primarily to keep Charlie from seriously injuring his wife. Charlie lets go of his wife and begins to struggle with you. By now Charlie has completely lost his cool and you find yourself becoming more aggressive out of necessity. You have finally pinned Charlie against the wall and are putting handcuffs on him when his wife and in-laws begin threatening to attack you. Although you have temporarily subdued Charlie you realize a new threat exists as his wife and in-laws become increasingly agitated.

You are alone and the situation is rapidly deteriorating. What are you going to do?

Based on what you have read, answer the following questions:

1. What options do you have in handling the situation? Which option will be the most effective?

2. If you had a partner, could the situation be handled differently?

3. What can the police do in "repeat calls" to help prevent them from occurring over and over again?

CASE 2

BETWEEN A ROCK AND
A HARD PLACE

You are a deputy sheriff in a small rural county. Your main duties are to serve court processes such as warrants, subpoenas, and court orders. The sheriff has called you to the office to pick up and serve a court order.

As you walk inside the sheriff's office, you notice a small-framed, dirty looking woman in her early thirties sitting in a chair. You know the woman because she has been on the arrest docket for everything from prostitution to child abuse.

The sheriff gives you a court order from the judge. The order is to be served on the woman's mother-in-law. You ask the sheriff what the court order concerns and he explains that apparently the woman's small child was being treated for a minor illness at the hospital and the woman's mother-in-law came to the hospital and picked the child up without permission. The sheriff further explained that the woman's mother-in-law refused to return the child to his mother. The sheriff advises you to serve the court order on the mother-in-law. He further advises that "a lady from Human Services will meet you at the scene to take custody of the child."

The court order sickens you. You feel that the woman may only want the child back to get back at her mother-in-law. Based on her previous behavior, you feel the woman is an unfit mother, but the court seems reluctant to remove the child from her care and supervision. The woman's husband left her when the baby was born and the mother-in-law has tried to take custody of the child on several occasions. In fact, the woman and the mother-in-law have been fighting over the child for three years.

You know that the woman is using the law and you to get the child back. The woman does not seem to have any real concern for the well-being of the child and appears to want only the extra welfare money she receives. You know the woman's mother-in-law will not give the child up easily. You even hope that the mother-in-law and child will not be at home when you arrive with the court order.

As you arrive at the mother-in-law's home, you can see the child peering out a window. While knocking on the front door, you glance back and notice the Human Services representative arriving with the mother.

"Why the hell did she bring the mother over here?" you mumble to yourself. The mother-in-law comes to the door and becomes increasingly angry as you try to explain that you have a court order and must take the child and return it to its mother.

The mother-in-law begins to explain the reasons she took the child. She tells you the mother had not taken proper care of the child. She tells you the child was sick and malnourished. She adds that the hospital had treated the child for a severe chest cold and that she had taken the child in order to clothe and feed it. You know that the mother-in-law is probably right, but you also feel that you have no choice but to pick the child up and return it to its mother.

The mother-in-law picks up an old single-barrel shotgun from behind the door and points it at you. She tells you that she will kill you before letting the child go back to the mother.

The mother-in-law is getting very upset and begins to cry. Pointing the shotgun, she threatens the child's mother with violence. The child's mother begins to yell at you and her mother-in-law. The mother-in-law is becoming increasingly upset. The Human Services lady looks surprised and indecisive.

The child in question is also beginning to cry.

Based on what you have read, answer the following questions:
1. What should you do at this point?
2. Can you legally do anything to prevent the mother from taking custody of her child?
3. What would have been the best course of action to start with?

CASE 3
POLICE OFFICER OR SOCIAL WORKER?

Jack and Ann Smith are a married couple with three children ranging in age from five months to six years. Jack is unemployed and is 60 percent disabled from a wound he received in Vietnam. Ann has to provide primary care for the children and also has a part-time job at a nearby grocery store. Jack and Ann live in a housing project where the rent is based on the government welfare checks they receive.

It is near the end of the month and the food stamps have almost been depleted. Jack spent what little money they had left on beer for himself and his friends. Over the years, Jack has continued to feel bitter about his disability and apparently tries to drown his problems with alcohol.

Jack and Ann had an argument earlier in the day over the amount of money Jack spends on beer and wine. Ann was also becoming increasingly upset over Jack frequenting bars and not trying to help with household responsibilities and chores. Ann even accused Jack of feeling sorry for himself and of being a failure in general. Jack responded by slapping Ann several times and leaving the house in a fit of temper.

While Jack was gone, the two eldest children began fighting with each other, which resulted in the youngest child crying. Although Ann had carefully cleaned the apartment the day before, the children had again made a mess of the house. Her patience wearing thin, Ann rocked the youngest child in a rocking chair in an effort to stop his crying. After substantial threats from their mother, the two oldest children started playing in the kitchen and eventually broke several dishes that were on the table. That was the last straw! Ann began whipping the oldest child for breaking the dishes. Full of anger and frustration, she whipped the child so hard that he fainted and was apparently unconscious.

Jack came back to the apartment a short time later, intoxicated and still upset over the argument in which he and Ann had engaged earlier. He found the younger children crying, the oldest child badly beaten, and Ann sitting in a kitchen chair sobbing. In a fit of rage, Jack began beating Ann.

The next-door-neighbor, aware of what was happening, called the police and explained the situation.

You are a patrol officer assigned to the call. Your partner is a female officer with little police experience. Not knowing for sure what the situation is, you do not call for a backup car. In your opinion, at this point, it is a routine family disturbance call.

As you stand outside the Smiths' apartment door, you hear children sobbing. No one answers the door or speaks to you when you knock. You think to yourself, "These people need a social worker, not a police officer." Your partner looks at you, uncertain and waiting for instructions. You take a deep breath and try to decide what the best course of action will be.

Based on what you have read, answer the following questions:

1. What can you and your partner legally do?
2. What agencies other than the police could help in this situation?
3. How could the police become more proactively involved in these types of situations?

CASE 4
DIFFERENT CHOICES, EQUAL PROTECTION?

"You folks need to settle your differences and get along," Sergeant Waddell mumbles as he leaves the apartment with you trailing behind him.

The sergeant, a 30-year veteran, switches on the ignition of the cruiser and continues, half-talking to you and half-talking to himself.

"I don't know what the world's coming to! Two men living together like that. It just ain't natural. It's tough enough dealing with the Saturday night husband-and-wife drunks without having to try to calm down the likes of them. They like to call themselves gay, but from the looks of that smaller one, it don't look like he was having too gay of a time. Looked like that bigger feller whipped up on him. Besides, with him being thin like that, I wouldn't be surprised if he didn't have AIDS. I'll tell you one thing, I was glad to get out of there. Who knows what kind of germs was in their apartment?" Lighting a cigarette, he turns to you. "I bet they didn't teach you how to deal with those kind of people in college."

You pause before you respond, not wanting to offend the sergeant, who is also your training officer.

"We were taught that it would be difficult and challenging when dealing with the homosexual community because of AIDS, and our own biases and prejudices, as well as a lot of the myths that are going around."

"Myths, my ass," Sergeant Waddell interrupts. "That AIDS disease will kill you stone-cold dead. I don't trust the government. You can't tell me you can't catch that stuff from mosquitos either. Who knows how you can catch it? All I know is I want to wash my hands."

"Well, I would agree that there are a lot of questions," you reply. "But our professors always reminded us that every citizen was entitled to equal protection under the law, regardless of their sexual preference. I was taught that I was to treat them professionally, just as in any domestic disturbance. It seems to me that we should have done something besides just telling them to quiet down and get along with each other. I mean, we should have arrested the big guy just like we would have done it if was a spousal abuse case."

Turning into McDonald's, the sergeant turns once more to you. "Simpson, you're a good kid and I believe you will make a fine officer. But you need to remember that the classroom is one thing and the real world is another. I don't hate those kind of people, but they made their bed and now they'll have to lie in it. I don't know what else we could have done. They weren't married and, even if they were, I don't believe it's legal in this state. We couldn't take the little guy to a spousal abuse shelter, they'd laugh their asses off at us. And I don't think the domestic violence law covers people like that anyway. Why don't you go order us a couple of black coffees to go while I wash my hands?"

Waiting on the coffee, you reflect on Waddell's words. He is a respected veteran police officer and you understand his uneasiness. You felt it, too. You also remember the look of fear and helplessness on the face of the battered guy, Eddie, who called the police. One part of you wanted to go back and check on him and do something, even if it meant arresting the other guy for domestic violence. Another part of you wanted to stay on Sergeant Waddell's good side. After all, he is your training officer. What are you going to do?

Based on what you have read, answer the following questions:

1. What are the domestic violence laws in your state? How do homosexual relationships fit into the law of your state?

2. Should homosexual relationships be covered under domestic violence and spousal abuse laws? Why or why not?

3. What should you do in this case? Use your own state laws to jusify your actions.

CASE 5
HONOR THY FATHER AND MOTHER

As you park your cruiser next to the curb on Meadowview Street, you glance at your watch . . . just about the time you should be going on that coffee break you planned two hours ago. However, two traffic accidents and a drunken bar patron later, you still haven't managed to get the caffeine "boost" you've come to rely on for the night shift.

You can clearly see a portly woman who looks to be in her fifties standing anxiously in her driveway awaiting your arrival. She must be Mrs. Simms, who called 911. Leaving your cruiser, you introduce yourself.

"Ma'am, I'm Officer Smith. What seems to be the problem?" The woman, who is obviously quite anxious, replies in a loud whisper as she looks over her right shoulder at the house next to hers.

"Officer, I'm really scared for my neighbors, the McGillicutys. Ned is in his eighties and his wife, Mildred, is in her late seventies. I heard her scream several times tonight after dinner. My husband told me it was none of our business and maybe he's right . . . but I just can't live with myself if I stand by any longer and let it continue." Mrs. Simms begins to cry softly.

Patiently you respond, "Let what continue, Mrs. Simms?"

"The beatings," she replies in a choked voice.

After another five minutes of conversation with Mrs. Simms, you have a pretty good picture of what is going on. The McGillicutys had moved in with their divorced son, in his mid-forties, apparently at his request. Mr. McGillicuty had not fully recovered from a stroke six months ago and was, for the most part, bedridden. The son, Bob, had begun to drink heavily. For the last two months, according to Mrs. Simms, he had been progressively abusing his parents, particularly his mother.

You radio in the information to headquarters and are advised that the dispatcher is contacting the state department of social services. A few minutes later, the dispatcher advises that an APS worker is en route to meet you at the McGillicutys' residence. APS, or Adult Protective Services, is a unit similar to Child Protective Services but with a focus on the needs of the elderly and elderly abuse.

You park your cruiser in front of the McGillicutys' house and wait for the arrival of the social worker. While waiting, you notice someone peering out the window of the McGillicutys' house. About twenty minutes later, a car with the familiar state emblem on the door pulls in behind your cruiser.

"Hi, I'm Ann Sheridan with APS."

"Ben Smith. You on call tonight?" you ask, while shaking Ann's hand.

"Yeah, my turn. The dispatcher said you might have an abused elderly woman here?"

You explain what the neighbor had told you as both you and Ann walk to the front entrance to the McGillicutys' house. After you have knocked repeatedly, the front door finally opens, revealing a frightened, elderly woman. There is a large red welt under her left eye, and she is gingerly holding her right wrist.

"Mrs. McGillicuty, I'm Officer Ben Smith and this is Social Services Counselor Ann Sheridan. We understand that you might be in need of assistance."

"Oh, no, Officer," Mrs. McGillicuty replies quickly, "I fell down the basement stairs, but I will be all right. I do appreciate your concern . . ."

You hear her words, but her look tells you much more. You have seen that look too many times. It was the same blank, hidden stare of fear and pain you had seen on the faces of many battered children and women. Before you have a chance to say anything else, a belligerent voice bellows, "Who the hell is at the door?"

From the kitchen emerges a middle-aged man who appears to be over six feet tall and weighing about 230 pounds. He has a partially empty beer bottle in his hand and walks with some degree of unsteadiness. You and Ann take advantage of the moment's confusion and step inside the front door to get a better look inside. The interior of the house is unkempt. Old newspapers are spread around the floor and empty beer bottles indicate that serious problems exist in the McGillicuty family. The son, Bob, addresses you and Ann. "We didn't call for the police. Everything is fine here. I bet it was that nosey neighbor, Mrs. Simms. Hey, you want a cold beer, officer? How about you, honey?"

As the son rambles on, you notice Mrs. McGillicuty hanging on her son's every word. When he finishes his beer and his "everything is fine" speech, his mother quickly backs up everything he had said.

"How is Mr. McGillicuty doing?" You interject.

"He's fine," the son quickly replies.

"Mind if we take a look?" Ann asks.

"Sure, go ahead," Bob replied, "I think I'll get me another beer. Sure you two don't want one?"

"No thanks," you and Ann simultaneously reply as you follow Mrs. McGillicuty to the father's room.

When you enter the bedroom, the stench is almost unbearable, although it doesn't seem to affect Mrs. McGillicuty. Mr. McGillicuty's eyes are closed.

He looks like he is in a coma. From the light of the bedside lamp, you can see that he and his bed need changing. You are thinking to yourself, "At least the old fellow doesn't know what's happening," when upon closer inspection you notice a single tear running down his left cheek. Ann takes out a small camera from her purse and tries to inconspicuously take a few photos.

Mrs. McGillicuty tugs on your sleeve and implores you not to report what you have seen.

"Officer Smith, please don't get the wrong impression. Bob isn't a bad boy. He's our only son and we love him. With his delicate emotional balance, any more problems could push him over the edge. He doesn't mean to be rude on occasion, but it's just his nature. I just wish I could be a better mother. If anything ever happened to him, I just don't know what we'd do . . . ," she says, her voice trailing off in a muffled sob.

You and Ann return to the living room and find Bob sitting in a recliner, smoking a cigarette and holding a fresh beer. "Bob, how'd your mother get that bruise on her face and hurt her wrist?" Ann asks.

"What did she tell you?" Bob responds.

"She said she fell down the stairs. Doesn't look like the kind of bruises one would get from falling down stairs though, does it?" Ann replies.

"Of course she fell. Hell, she's old. She bruises easily. You fell, didn't you, mommy?" Bob asks in a sarcastic manner.

Mrs. McGillicuty nods her head nervously.

You look at Ann and can see the frustration in her face. You know that had these two people been children, you could take immediate legal action. Unfortunately, child protection laws and spousal abuse laws do not pertain to elderly abuse.

"Ben, I might be able to get a court order on Mr. McGillicuty and have him committed to the state as an incompetent. I might even be able to get home health services out here for him. But I'm concerned more for Mrs. McGillicuty. Unless she wants to press charges on abuse, we can't do anything," Ann whispers to you.

Ann says her goodbyes and leaves to file her report. You stay behind to have a final word with Bob and Mrs. McGillicuty. You make it clear that you will be checking on them from time to time. Walking to your cruiser, you feel a knot in your stomach. "Those people don't deserve a son like that." Muttering to yourself, you start your cruiser; it's time for that coffee.

Based on what you have read, answer the following questions:

1. What are the laws in your state pertaining to protection of the elderly and elderly abuse?

2. How can the police and social services work together to help in cases of elderly abuse?

3. As the officer in this case, what would be your options? What action would you take?

CASE 6
THE COLOR OF A LIVING ROOM

You are a female police officer. You have worked for the police department a little over two years as a juvenile officer and have transferred into the patrol division only a few weeks ago. You enjoyed working in the juvenile bureau but felt you had greater career potential as a patrol officer. Some of the male patrol officers seemed a little apprehensive for one reason or another when you transferred into the patrol division. You had expected some resistance but believed that you could eventually prove yourself, which is what has happened. You currently have an older male partner, who works well with you and has made your transition much smoother.

You and your partner have just finished eating dinner when you receive a radio call about a family disturbance. As you proceed toward the address, you think about the training you received concerning how to handle family disputes. As your patrol car comes to a stop in front of the house in question, you can hear screaming and shouting coming from inside. After quickly surveying the surrounding area, your partner looks through the front porch window and observes a middle-aged couple having an argument. The screaming diminishes when your partner knocks on the front door and announces your presence.

A battered, middle-aged man comes to the door and asks if he can help you. He has a large bruise on the left side of his face, and his right eye is almost swollen shut. He looks embarrassed. Your partner introduces you and himself and asks if it is all right to enter the house and talk.

You follow the man and your partner into the living room, and you see the woman sitting on a sofa. The living room is a mess. There are paint cans, brushes, and newspapers strewn around the floor. It is obvious that the couple is in the process of painting the living room. You ask the woman what's going on, and she quickly becomes belligerent. She has obviously been drinking and is quite intoxicated. She explains to you that she wanted light blue paint in the living room, but her husband started painting the room a beige color. The woman suddenly rises from the sofa and begins to stumble around the room, cursing her husband all the while. The husband apologizes to you for his wife's behavior. He tells you that he was painting the living room when his wife came home from a friend's house after apparently having too much too drink. He further explains that he is afraid his wife may be becoming an alcoholic and that he is worried about her. That comment infuriates his wife even more.

Picking up a paint roller, she begins to threaten her husband. You step toward the woman in an effort to quiet her down. She unexpectedly swings the roller at you, hitting you on the arm and splattering paint over your uniform.

Your partner quickly relieves the woman of her paint roller and firmly orders her to settle down. After assessing and discussing the situation, you and your partner both agree that the husband probably needs medical attention. You also realize that if the husband were the violent party instead of the wife, he would be arrested. However, the husband assures you and your partner that he is all right and pleads with you not to arrest his wife.

Based on what you have read, answer the following questions:

1. What should you and your partner do?
2. How would the situation be different if the violent person were the husband instead of the wife?
3. What might you do to facilitate them getting the help that they need?

CASE 7
PUBLIC DUTY OR BROTHERHOOD?

You are a young police officer in a small town. You have worked for the police department for almost nine months. In four weeks you will be off probationary status and will be eligible for a salary increase.

You grew up in the town for which you work. Both you and your family are well liked and respected by most members of the community. You know many families in your town and feel you have a good relationship with most of them.

One night on patrol you receive a domestic disturbance call. From the dispatcher's remarks, you realize it is apparently a family fight complaint which was turned in by a neighbor.

Upon arriving at the scene, you notice that several of the neighbors have gathered in the front yard of the house. As you get out of your vehicle you can hear loud arguing coming from inside the house.

As you walk toward the house you advise the people in the yard that they should return to their homes. A couple of people voice objections and demand to know how you are going to handle the call. One man states, "He won't do anything to a fellow cop!"

You did not recognize the address as being a police officer's home, but you do recognize the car in the carport as one you have seen in the police parking lot. You now realize that a police officer does live here. You do not know the officer very well because he works a different shift than you do. However, you do know his name is Jason and that he has been on the force for about five years.

As you knock on the door of the house you glance behind you at the people still standing in the front yard. They are wondering and waiting to see how you will handle the situation. After the third knock, Jason opens the door. You smell beer and can see Jason has been drinking heavily.

Jason belligerently asks what you want. You explain that a neighbor has complained about the argument he is having with his wife. Jason's wife suddenly runs to the door and demands that you take Jason out of the house. Jason turns around, slaps her hard on the face, and then pushes her back into the house. You start inside and Jason turns to you and tells you to keep out of his and his wife's business. "I don't need no rookie to tell me how to run my private life," yells Jason. He sees the people standing in the front yard and screams at them to go away or he will throw them all in jail.

You are thinking to yourself that if Jason was not a police officer, you would not be as hesitant regarding your next move. Had he been any other person, you would already have put him in the back of your cruiser, heading to jail. But Jason is a fellow police officer. You have never had to handle a call involving another police officer before. You have heard from the other officers in the department how police officers have to take care of themselves, like a fraternity. You have previously let other officers off for minor speeding violations and such because they were fellow police officers. You have even gotten out of a few tickets yourself for the same reason. But this is a different situation. Private citizens are watching how you are going to handle this particular call.

You quickly step inside the house and close the door. Jason shouts, "I told you to get away from here." You see Jason's wife, sitting on the floor, sobbing. She has obviously been beaten.

You ask Jason for an explanation. Jason tells you there is nothing you can do except leave him alone. Jason's wife then shouts at you to take Jason to jail because she is afraid of him. Jason tells her to shut up, that no officer would put another police officer in jail.

You get Jason into the living room and have him sit on the couch. Using as much tact as you can, you explain the problem to Jason and urge him to calm down. After talking with Jason a few minutes, he becomes more subdued. Jason's wife is still upset and wants you to arrest Jason.

You look out the living room window and see even more people gathered outside. You know that some type of action must be taken. If you arrest Jason, you will defuse the crowd outside as well as temporarily protect Jason's wife from further abuse. If you do not arrest Jason, you may contribute to a serious problem between the community, yourself, and the police department. You may also lose your job. Jason will more than likely lose his job if he is arrested. You are still looking out the window at the crowd of people waiting for you to take action. They want you to arrest a fellow police officer. Either way you go, you are going to have some problems.

Based on what you have read, answer the following questions:

1. What steps should you take to alleviate the problems with (a) the crowd outside, (b) Jason, and (c) Jason's wife? Explain what impact your solutions will have on police-community relations.

2. How will the community view their local police if (a) you arrest Jason or (b) you do not arrest Jason?

3. How will the other members of the police department view this encounter? How would they react if Jason were arrested? If Jason were a police officer with another law enforcement agency, would there be a difference?

CASE 8
DOUBLE BIND

You have been working patrol with your partner, Jim, for more than three years, and you have never seen him this anxious when answering a domestic disturbance call.

"Jim, are you all right?" you ask.

"Yeah, I'll be OK. Probably some indigestion from eating that taco," Jim responds, popping another antacid in his mouth.

The last time you saw Jim this nervous was when his wife left him a year and a half ago. Because you are a woman, Jim sought your advice then. Over countless cups of coffee, Jim had eventually confessed to you what you already had known—that the reason his wife left him was because he had run around on her one time too many.

For the last three months, Jim has seemed more settled and upbeat. He has indicated to you on several occasions that his new girlfriend has made "a new man" out of him. Whatever her effect, you have to agree that Jim has a more positive attitude about his work and his life. For that, you are grateful. The three of you even had lunch together last week.

As you and Jim approached the residence, you could hear shouting inside. You could also see the neighbors who had reported the disturbance peering out of their upstairs window.

After you announce yourself as the police and knock loudly on the door several times, the noise inside calms down and a man, red-faced and obviously upset, opens the door. After you and Jim step inside the house, your jaw almost hits the floor. The wife with the tear-streaked face is none other than Jim's current girlfriend, Jane. When you turn to look at your partner, he averts his eyes. Not sure what to do, you decide to take Jane into an adjoining bedroom and ask Jim to talk with her husband in the living room. Jane is obviously embarrassed and continues to repeat over and over again, "I'm sorry." After you calm her down, you leave her sitting on the side of the bed and return to the living room, where you find her husband apologizing to a subdued Jim for upsetting the neighbors.

"I'm sorry for everything, officers. I just found out that my wife has been running around on me. We've been married for ten years and have a six-year-old son, who is over at his grandmother's. I got so angry when I found out that I lost my temper. If I could find the sorry bastard who's been trying to break up our family, you would probably have to arrest me for assault and battery!"

You and Jim ride in silence back to the precinct station. You volunteer to write up the report and Jim nods in agreement as he quickly excuses himself.

Pulling the tab on a diet soft drink, you take a long drink from the can and reflect on your relationship with your partner and the report you are about to write.

Based on what you have read, answer the following questions:

1. Should the officer in question discuss Jim's inappropriate behavior with him, with her supervisor, or should she simply ignore the incident?

2. How has Jim's conduct compromised his professional role as a police officer?

3. What kind of counseling services might benefit Jim or his partner in a situation such as this one? Is the police agency responsible for providing such services?

Section III

THE POLICE AND JUVENILES

Introduction

The majority of police contact with juveniles comes after they get involved in some antisocial or delinquent behavior. Because of this limited contact, police officers may perceive many juveniles as either delinquent or potentially delinquent. Therefore, it is easy for an officer to develop negative attitudes toward juveniles in general. Most police officers realize that a large number of adult offenders have juvenile offense records. This factor also increases the negative attitudes of police officers toward juvenile offenders.

The juvenile justice system is a separate and distinct system from the adult criminal justice system. Juvenile offenders do not commit crimes, they commit delinquent acts. Therefore, police officers must handle juveniles much differently than adults. Many police officers are apprehensive about the juvenile justice system. Officers often view juvenile justice in the same light as criminal justice. The philosophy of juvenile justice maintains that it is different from criminal justice. Nevertheless, police officers frequently become irritated and frustrated when they see a juvenile "get off easy" for a crime that would send an adult to prison. Police officers are also directly or indirectly involved in the assistance, aid, and counseling of juveniles (Hirschi and Goffredson, 1993).

Police officers are expected in many cases to counsel potentially delinquent juveniles. Many police agencies and juvenile court agencies utilize off-duty police officers on a voluntary basis as "guidance counselors" for misguided youth. This follows the same philosophy as the juvenile courts in that juvenile offenders need help or guidance rather than punishment.

The Philosophy of the Juvenile Justice System

Courts and law have been inclined to take a special attitude toward juveniles who commit offenses. Under the English Common Law, a child under the age of seven could not be convicted of a crime. The child was regarded as not responsible and not chargeable with the offense. For children between the ages of seven and fourteen, the common law presumed that a child was not responsible for an offense but was open to review by the court to determine if the child had enough intelligence to realize the act was wrong. Because many of these children could pass the test, it was not uncommon for them to be sentenced to long penitentiary terms or to death.

During the nineteenth century, public opinion changed and turned against imprisoning young children with hardened adult criminals. Reformatories and training schools were developed for the detention, education, and rehabilitation of young offenders. Special courts were established along with procedures for dealing with delinquent youth. To carry out the philosophy of care and protection rather than punishment, these courts were given jurisdiction over dependent and neglected children as well. In most states the juvenile court handles cases involving juveniles below the age of eighteen. If the juvenile offender has committed a serious offense, such as murder, the juvenile court may waive jurisdiction and send the child to an adult criminal court providing the child meets age requirements. Theoretically, a juvenile offender is not prosecuted and there is no conviction. The state is not trying to punish the offender but is trying to find out what is wrong and how to deal with it in a way that is beneficial for the child as well as the public (Whitehead and Lab, 2002). As a result, the juvenile court is usually informal and private, although more recently appellate and Supreme Court decisions have made the procedure more formalized in order to protect the child's due process rights.

The Police Officer's View of Juvenile Offenders

It is often difficult for police officers to accept the juvenile court's point of view regarding juvenile offenders. The juvenile court is committed to the viewpoint of aiding a juvenile offender, even those who are serious and repeat offenders. The laws applying to juvenile offenders are designed to help the youth as much as possible without subjecting the community to threat of danger or disruption. Many police officers are often frustrated by what appears to them to be the juvenile court letting juvenile criminals go free and unpunished. As a result, police officers are inclined to feel uncomfortable in dealing with juvenile offenders because of the philosophy of the juvenile justice system.

There is a fine line that exists between delinquent behavior and delinquent criminal behavior which is not always clear and often confusing for police officers. Many offenses for which a juvenile may be arrested are not offenses for adults. Possession of alcoholic beverages, running away from home, and violation of curfew are offenses for juveniles and are, thus, status offenses. Delinquent criminal acts are offenses for which an adult could also be arrested. Therefore, many police officers become apprehensive toward making arrests of juveniles committing status offenses. Police officers may feel that such juvenile offenders would be "better off" when punished by their parents or a referral agency rather than bringing formal charges in juvenile court. In this respect, police officers have a great deal of discretionary flexibility when dealing with juveniles. The appropriate use of this flexibility may not only prevent the stigma of labeling a juvenile a delinquent but may also prevent the juvenile's behavior from progressing to adult criminal offenses.

The Juvenile's View of Police Officers

The police officer has one important negative barrier to overcome even before contact is made with a juvenile: to most juveniles, a police officer is the symbol of bad experiences with other authority figures including fathers, mothers, and teachers. As a result, the police officer may become a victim of displacement, where the negative attitude juveniles have toward other authority figures becomes focused on the officer.

When a juvenile, in the presence of his or her peer group, is approached by a police officer, he/she may react in a disrespectful, "tough" manner. Norms of a juvenile's peer group can create a view of the police as foes, and disrespect may be demonstrated by refusing to be "shoved around" or "clamming up" when police officers ask questions. Therefore, it is important that police officers recognize that any relationship formed with a juvenile will, to a large extent, be dependent upon the officer's manner of approach, the officer's ability to communicate, and the impact of peers present at the interaction.

Police officers who approach a juvenile in a negative manner immediately decrease the possibility for any positive relationship or communication with the juvenile. Police officers who use excessive authority and adopt overbearing attitudes are communicating disrespect to a juvenile and will find it very difficult to gain the trust or confidence of the youth in question. Juvenile mistrust of police officers may even continue into adulthood. Juveniles are often very sensitive to the insecurities and attitudes of adults in general and may be able to detect even the slightest amount of deception.

Juveniles often interpret events quite differently than do adults. For instance, an adult who receives a speeding citation may dismiss it as bad luck being caught, whereas a juvenile who receives a ticket may experience substantial fear of being cited, including significant dread of any punitive consequences. The juvenile may also perceive the officer's speeding citation as a form of harassment. In addition, some police officers refuse to give the same consideration to juveniles as they do to adults. When this occurs, juveniles often perceive such differential treatment as discrimination.

Policing Juvenile Offenders

When police officers detect an offense by a juvenile, a discretionary judgement is usually made. The juvenile offender may either be diverted from the juvenile justice process or be taken into custody. Two-thirds of the juveniles who come into contact with the police are handled informally (Wilson and Howell, 1994; Whitehead and Lab, 2002). Informal handling may include verbal reprimands, counseling with the youth and his/her parents, or referral to a community agency for treatment. Formal handling involves official arrest, detention, and court appearances.

Diversion is a commonly used approach when dealing with juvenile offenders. Diversion usually consists of an agreement between the juvenile, the parents, and the police, which includes referral to a community helping agency and informal probation. With such arrangements, the juvenile typically reports to a probation officer on a scheduled basis (Hirschi and Goffredson, 1993).

Generally, the legal standards for juvenile offenders are broader than those for adult arrests. Whereas the probable cause standard is used in adult arrest, police officers have more discretion in determining if juvenile offenders fall under the jurisdiction of the juvenile court (Whitehead and Lab, 2002). Discretion of arrest in juvenile cases has both positive and negative aspects. The flexibility given police officers in decision making can be beneficial, but this flexibility can be misused and indiscriminately applied to an individual juvenile.

Studies of police arrest patterns indicate that several factors are important in determining whether a juvenile offender is handled formally or informally. The most influential factor in the arrest decision process seems to be the severity of the offense (Piliavin and Briar, 1964; Wilson and Howell, 1994). Serious offenses are generally handled formally by the police. The number of prior contacts a juvenile offender has had with the police, the social status of the juvenile, the race of the juvenile, the age of the juvenile, and the juvenile offender's general attitude and demeanor are all additional factors influencing whether the police handle the juvenile offender formally or informally (Thurman, Zhao, and Giacomazzi, 2001; Whitehead and Lab, 2002). When police officers handle juvenile offenders in a formal manner, the practice follows procedures similar to those for adults. Court decisions have established due process guidelines for juvenile offenders along the same general lines as due process rights of adults (Fox, 1984; Whitehead and Lab, 2002).

The Police and Child Abuse

The police and the juvenile justice system play very critical roles in the problem of child abuse. Child abuse not only includes the physical battering and mistreatment of children but also neglect. A wide range of behavior may be defined as child abuse. Abuse may include physical, emotional, medical, educational, and moral forms of neglect. Physical neglect relates to environmental conditions in which a child may be confined. The physical condition of the child's home where dirt and a lack of sanitation exists is considered physical neglect. In addition, improper care for a child such as inadequate clothing or lack of food constitutes physical neglect. Emotional neglect involves the failure of parents to provide adequate emotional support for a child. Medical neglect occurs when the parents do not provide necessary medical treatment to correct a condition from which a child suffers. Educational neglect may occur when the parent fails to make a child available for school as required by state statutes. Moral neglect occurs when the child is subjected to immoral influences which may be corruptive.

Even with increased legal authority for police officers, teachers, and physicians to act on behalf of abused children, the courts have often been reluctant to remove children from such environments (Dyke, 1980; Smith and Meyer, 1984). One of the major problems is the definition of child abuse and neglect. Although one can label the types of abuse and neglect as moral, physical, emotional, educational, and medical, it is sometimes difficult to determine where to draw the line. What is considered physical abuse by one person may be considered proper control by another. The courts are reluctant to break apart families by removing children unless the abuse is very serious or if charges of abuse have been brought before the court previously. By the same token, police officers are reluctant to interfere with the parents' control of their children. The difference in perception of child abuse by juvenile court judges and vague laws regarding child abusive parents creates a sense of apprehensiveness for police officers acting on suspected child abuse cases (Erez and Tontodonato, 1989).

There is concern over the increasing reports of child sexual exploitation and molestation. Child sexual abuse, incest and exploitation cases are often difficult for police to discover. Many child sexual molesters are nonviolent, respected members of the community. In most cases, the exploiting adult, the child victim, and, often the parents of the victim conspire in silence for mutual protection from the police and criminal justice system (Caplan, 1982; Whitcomb et al., 1994). The discovery and/or reporting of child sexual abuse is typically by accident and often not due to any rigorous investigative efforts. For example, it appears that in father-daughter incest cases, the mother may often be aware of the problem and may even support the practice (Ward, 1985).

Summary

Police officers have a unique impact on juveniles' attitudes. How a police officer relates to a juvenile has a significant impact on the type of attitude the youth will have toward law enforcement in general for years to come. It is important for police officers to realize that they are usually the first contact a juvenile has with "the system." The difference between the juvenile justice system and the criminal justice system provides an avenue of discretion for police officers dealing with juvenile offenders.

Because the philosophy of the juvenile justice system is focused on the care and protection of the child, the police are allowed to utilize the same philosophy in their dealings with juveniles. This philosophy not only provides broader discretion for police officers but also allows for broader action by police officers in trying to help correct problem juveniles. Police officers and other officials have broad authority under the law to act on suspected cases of child abuse and neglect. Therefore, police officers are not only acting as representatives of the law with juveniles but also can provide a social service or helping function when interacting with youth.

References

Caplan, G. (1982). "Sexual Exploitation of Children," *Police Magazine*, January.

Dyke, E. V. (1980). "Child Abuse," *New York Teacher*, May 18.

Erez, E., and P. Tontodonato. (1989). "Patterns of Reported Parent-Child Abuse and Police Response." *Journal of Family Violence*, 4(2): 143–159.

Fox, S. (1984). *The Law of Juvenile Courts in a Nutshell*, 3d ed. St. Paul: West Publishing Co.

Hirschi, T., and M. Goffredson. (1993). "Rethinking the Juvenile Justice System." *Crime and Delinquency*, 39(2): 262–271.

Piliavin, I., and S. Briar. (1964). "Police Encounters with Juveniles," *American Journal of Sociology*, September.

Senna, J., and L. Siegel. (1981). *Juvenile Delinquency: Theory, Practice and Law*. St. Paul: West Publishing Co.

Smith, S. R., and R. G. Meyer. (1984). "Child Abuse Reporting Laws and Psychotherapy: A Time for Reconsideration," *International Journal of Law and Psychiatry*, 7(3–4): 351–366.

Thurman, Q., J. Zhao, and A. Giacomazzi. (2001). *Community Policing in a Community Era*. Los Angeles: Roxbury Publishing Co.

Ward, E. (1985). *Father-Daughter Rape*. New York: Grove Press.

Whitcomb, D., G. Goodman, D. Runyan, and S. Hoak. (1994). "The Emotional Effects of Testifying in Sexually Abused Children." *Research in Action*, April. Washington, DC: National Institute of Justice.

Whitehead, J., and S. Lab. (2002). *Introduction to Juvenile Justice*, 2d ed. Cincinnati: Anderson Publishing Co.

Wilson, J., and J. Howell. (1994). "Serious and Violent Juvenile Crime: A Comprehensive Strategy." *Juvenile and Family Court Journal*, 45(2): 3–14.

CASES INVOLVING JUVENILES

The impact the police have on juveniles is largely determined by the attitude and personal conduct of the individual officer. Every police officer must bear in mind that he or she is not only a representative of the law but may also have to fulfill social service functions when interacting with juveniles.

In dealing with a younger child or older juvenile who has violated the law, the police officer is often the child's first official contact with the system. Many times he or she takes on the additional responsibilities of being prosecutor, judge, and correctional representative as well. There are thousands of cases each year in which youths are unofficially counseled by police officers. These officers exert considerable influence, for better or worse, in the lives of juveniles with whom they come in contact.

Case number one, "I Sorry, Officer," explores a situation common among lower socioeconomic-class juveniles. A police officer is faced with not only a law enforcement matter, but one that brings the officer to a face-to-face reality with the problems of the poor.

Case number two, "Neighborhood Brat," examines a police officer interacting with the parents of a juvenile offender. It is sometimes difficult for parents to understand that their children are not always what they view them to be. In this case, the parents of a young boy refuse to believe that their son can commit delinquent acts.

Case number three, "Boy with a Gun," focuses on an increasing problem of crimes committed on school property. A police officer must decide how to handle a principal, parents, and a young boy accused of carrying a firearm to school. The firearm is an antique rifle to be used for a class demonstration, but the principal is adamant about pressing charges on a technical basis.

Case number four, "Cruisers," portrays a situation where the age-old problem of teenage automobile cruising is creating problems for merchants, shoppers, and, ultimately, the police. A police sergeant is given the opportunity to provide input on how the problem might be resolved.

Case number five, "Right Side of the Tracks, Wrong Side of the Law," deals with a group of upper middle-class teenagers involved in drug dealing and vandalism. A deputy sheriff must decide what he will recommend to the judge. The sheriff wants the case dismissed; the D.A. wants blood.

Case number six, "Homegrown Terrorism," explores the difficulties police officers face when dealing with modern teenagers and their parents. Teenagers are very impressionable and often act out the prejudicial attitudes of their parents. What a parent may express as a bias, a teenager may take literally. In this case, an elderly Arabic American has been terrorized and assaulted, and the officers try to get the parents to understand the seriousness of their sons' assault.

Case number seven, "A Loving Father?" examines the problem of father-daughter incest. A police officer and social worker must investigate two young girls' accusations of incest by their father.

Case number eight, "Welcome Home?", involves the legal and emotional concerns of a police officer dealing with runaways. The officer finds that while locating and returning juvenile runaways to their parents is a police responsibility, the circumstances surrounding the runaway act may be more important.

CASE 1
"I SORRY, OFFICER"

You are a police officer assigned to patrol in an urban residential area. Your beat is a lower socioeconomic area comprised of housing projects, small stores, and warehouses. You are currently working the day shift.

While cruising down Elm Street, you routinely pull into a grocery store parking lot. Sometimes you are able to find stolen automobiles that have been abandoned in various public parking lots. As you begin to check a car with no license plates, you notice a small boy running between the parked cars. The boy appears to be attempting to hide from you. You get out of your patrol car and walk over to where the boy is hiding. You find the boy squatting behind one of the cars. He could be no more than seven or eight years old and is carefully guarding a large shopping bag he has in his possession.

You ask the boy where his mother is, thinking that a parent would not be far from such a small child. He quickly informs you that his mother is working at a factory two blocks away. The boy further explains that his father does not live with him and his mother anymore. He goes on to explain that his name is David and that he lives alone with his mother in a project several blocks away.

You look into the shopping bag and find that it contains C.B. radios, tape players, and other items commonly found in automobiles. You ask David where he got the contents of the bag and he tells you he found them. David is unable to explain to you where he found the items. You pick up the shopping bag, take David by the hand, and walk through the parking lot with him. You notice several cars with doors partially open and windows broken. Upon closer inspection, you find that they were apparently burglarized. Again, you ask David where he got the items in the shopping bag. David begins to cry and tells you he stole them from the cars in the parking lot.

You take David back to your patrol car and have him sit down in the front seat. By the way David is dressed you know he is poor. Sitting next to David in the car, you ask him what he was going to do with the stolen items. Still crying, he tells you about how he takes the stolen merchandise to a nearby high school and sells them to a teenage student. Apparently this is not the first time David has stolen things. David only knows the teenage fence by his first name, Willie. He tells you that Willie usually gives him a couple of dollars for the stolen items. It is obvious that Willie has a good racket going by buying several hundred dollars worth of goods for only a couple of dollars. Willie probably resells the items for three or four times the money he gives the small teary-eyed boy sitting in your cruiser. Seven-year-olds and teenagers! Your gut starts to ache as you wonder for a moment where it will stop, or if it, in fact, ever will.

David goes on to tell you that he only began stealing things a couple of weeks ago. He explains that he only wanted enough money to buy a birthday present for his mother next week. David says that his mother has not received a birthday present since his father left. He wants to buy his mother a new dress.

A lot of kids have lied to you before, but this time you believe what David is telling you. You feel sorry for him. Knowing that what action you take will have a lasting impression on the child makes you uncomfortable and frustrated. Generally, all you would have to do is turn David over to the juvenile authorities and let them handle the case. It sickens you to think about treating the child in a formal police manner. You could wait until the owners of the property returned to their cars, give the items back to them, and take David home. But David needs to learn right from wrong. He needs so many things. You wonder how many other Davids are stealing for Willie. You buy David a coke to buy yourself some time; you need to think. He looks up at you for an answer. Your cruiser's radio breaks the silence, "DWI on Elm Street. . . ."

Based on what you have read, answer the following questions:

1. What should you do?
2. Could you effectively handle the situation by yourself? What options do you have?
3. The young boy could be an effective link into a serious burglary-larceny problem. What is the problem and how could it be handled by the police?

CASE 2
NEIGHBORHOOD BRAT

You are a police officer assigned to the juvenile bureau and are presently responding to a request from a patrol officer to meet with you at a residence in the outskirts of the city.

As you pull up behind the patrol cruiser at the residence, a patrolman comes up to your car and tells you that he believes you should handle the situation inside. The patrolman explains that he answered a call to the Bakers' residence regarding an assault on the Bakers' twelve-year-old son. He states that the Bakers' next-door-neighbor, a Mr. Sutton, took a water hose and sprayed the Baker boy with it. Further explanation suggests that the Baker boy has been something of a troublemaker in the neighborhood. His previous escapades have included minor vandalism, fighting with other children, and generally being a nuisance to the neighborhood. In concluding his report, the patrolman laughs and tells you that he believes the boy probably "got off easy."

You approach the Baker house to talk with the parents. The boy's parents are visibly upset and insist that their son is very well mannered and that Mr. Sutton intentionally tried to harm their son. They further explain that their son has a cold and might well become seriously ill as a result of the incident. The Bakers are very angry and want to press charges against Mr. Sutton. Trying to be diplomatic, you advise the Bakers that you will talk with Mr. Sutton and will return shortly for further discussion with them.

You find Mr. Sutton in his back yard waxing his car. You introduce yourself and ask him what happened to the Baker boy. Mr. Sutton seems friendly and is quite cooperative in explaining his version of what happened. He contends that the Baker boy is always bothering people in the neighborhood by breaking windows, destroying gardens, and being a nuisance. Mr. Sutton goes on to explain that the boy came over while he was washing the car and started throwing dirt and mud on the car and running away. Finally, after warning the Bakers' son several times, he grabbed the boy and sprayed him with the water hose until he was soaking wet. After that the boy ran home crying. Mr. Sutton further informs

71

you that despite many complaints from the neighborhood, the Bakers treat their son as if he were always innocent and everyone else were lying.

Apparently, the Bakers are unable or unwilling to control their son. They appear to be overprotective and reinforce the child's behavior by not disciplining him. You are beginning to wonder whether the real problem is with the son or with his parents. Walking back to the Bakers' house, you must now decide what to tell them. It would be easier to advise the Bakers to take a warrant against Mr. Sutton and let the court handle the situation. On the other hand, the whole Baker family seems to need a different kind of help. You doubt they would be willing to commit themselves to family counseling, even if you tried to convince them it was needed. You mutter to yourself, "I am a police officer, not a psychologist."

You knock on the Bakers' front door, still undecided about what to tell them.

Based on what you have read, answer the following questions:
1. What should you say to the Bakers?
2. Should Mr. Sutton be prosecuted for his actions? Why or why not?
3. Could this matter be resolved in juvenile court? In civil court? Explain how either court could help the Bakers or be detrimental to them.

CASE 3
BOY WITH A GUN

You are a patrol officer responding to a call concerning a local high school. The dispatcher advised you that the school principal wanted to see a police officer.

Arriving at the principal's office, you are given directions to the guidance counselor's office. Upon entering the guidance counselor's office, you see the principal, the guidance counselor, and a young man approximately 15 years of age. The principal tells you that the young man, Charles Stinson, was apprehended with a gun in the hallway of the school. The principal seems rather excited, overbearing, and even intimidating, not only towards the boy but also towards you.

"Officer . . . uh . . . Baker," the principal addresses you as he pulls on your nameplate to read your name. "We will not tolerate any student on this campus carrying weapons. I don't need to tell you that problems such as this have been increasing over the past few years. This young man will be used as an example to all our students who may think about carrying weapons at my school."

"Yessir, I understand your concern . . . where is the gun?" you ask, looking around the office.

"I put it in the closet here for safekeeping. I don't know if it's ready to fire or not," the principal states, opening a closet door.

When the principal emerges, you chuckle aloud. The weapon is obviously an antique cap-and-ball black powder rifle.

"It's an 1859 Springfield .58 caliber Civil War musket," the young man states.

"You shut up, Stinson. I'll not have any of your insolence," the principal replies harshly.

"Excuse me, son . . . Charles, is it? Why did you bring this gun to school?" you ask the student.

"Why it's obvious, I think," the principal interrupts. "He's in need of mental help. He's trying to intimidate students and faculty . . . Why, he could have shot somebody! You know those stories about people with an AK-47 going into a place of work or school and shooting people."

"I hardly would put this gun in the same class of weapons as AK-47s," you respond, trying not to laugh.

"I was taking it to my American History class to show my classmates. We're studying the Civil War years and I thought I'd show my great-great-grandfather's rifle to the class," Stinson states.

"So you say. Well, now that Officer Baker is here, you'll be going to the juvenile detention center and I'll make it a point to have you expelled at the next school board meeting," the principal replies.

"Excuse me, Mr. Peters, you have a long-distance phone call in your office," a secretary interrupts, sticking her head through the door.

"I'll be back in a minute," the principal states as he exits the room.

You look over at the guidance counselor, who has been quiet the whole time.

"Is this guy for real? Does he really expect me to arrest this boy for carrying a Civil War rifle to school?" you ask, chuckling in bewilderment.

"Mr. Peters is . . . well, he's had some problems lately," the guidance counselor answers. "But he is the principal, and my boss. There's not much I can do to intervene. I will tell you that Mr. Stinson here is a straight-A student who has never been in trouble before. I took the liberty of calling his parents before you got here, and they're on the way down here. I believe they're pretty angry and upset that Mr. Peters is making such a fuss about this," the guidance counselor adds.

"Oh, boy," you think to yourself. The parents are on their way to school, already angry, and you are in the middle.

"Sorry for the interruption. Now, Officer Baker, are you ready to take custody of Mr. Stinson?" the principal asks as he re-enters the office.

"Look, Mr. Peters, this boy had an antique rifle that wasn't loaded and probably can't shoot anyway. He had no intention of using it to threaten or intimidate anyone. I don't think an arrest is warranted in this . . ."

"I don't care what you think, Officer Baker. State law is clear on this matter. Anyone bringing a firearm onto school property is committing a felony. This is a firearm and I expect you to uphold the law," the principal interrupts.

"Excuse me, Mr. Peters. Mr. and Mrs. Stinson are here and wanting to see you and their son," the secretary states, sticking her head through the office doorway again.

Based on what you have read, answer the following questions:
1. What are you going to tell Mr. Peters and the Stinsons in an effort to resolve the conflict now, even if it is temporary?
2. If an arrest were made, would it escalate into further problems or would it solve the immediate police problem?
3. If an arrest were made, what do you think the courts would do? What do you think the school board would do?
4. What kind of message would an arrest send to the other students enrolled in the high school?

CASE 4
CRUISERS

You are a patrol sergeant in a 116-officer police department. You are in charge of a patrol squad of nine officers in Zone 3. Zone 3 is a patrol deployment area consisting mostly of commercial establishments such as a mall, numerous restaurants, two four-lane highways, and three shopping centers. Zone 3 is considered to be one of the busiest areas of the city, particularly on the 4 P.M. to 12 A.M. shift.

One of the shopping centers has become increasingly popular with local high school students as a place to cruise. The shopping center has a movie theatre that draws numerous young people on weekend evenings.

Shoppers and especially managers of many of the stores in the shopping center have turned in repeated complaints over the past few months. Traffic is overwhelming on weekends due to teenagers cruising around the shopping center. There have been several minor assault cases, and shoplifting charges have increased as well. Drug sale activity has also been suspected in the area.

Your watch commander, under orders from the chief of police, has asked you to keep a highly visible presence around the shopping center—the assumption being that a visible police presence will deter teenagers from cruising the area. You found out quickly that the presence of your officers in the same area as the teenagers did not deter the teens but increased the potential for hostility between your officers and the cruisers. Officers who questioned the presence of teenagers at the shopping center got the usual response, "What are we doing wrong?" The entrance and egress roadways in the shopping center are considered public thoroughfares in your state, so trespassing laws do not apply to cruisers.

Your officers have made several arrests of juvenile offenders for possession of alcohol, drugs, and shoplifting. However, the increased arrests have not deterred the majority of the cruisers. You are aware that most of the young people out cruising the shopping center are law-abiding kids just out having fun. After all, it hasn't been that long since you went out cruising yourself as a high school student.

One day the watch commander calls you to headquarters.

"Jim, the chamber of commerce and the City Merchant's Association have pressured the city council on this cruising problem at Hillsdale Shopping Center. It seems the merchants are complaining that these kids are running off business and customers won't come in to shop with all the traffic there. The city council has passed a city ordinance against cruising which goes into effect the first of next month," Captain Adams explains.

"Captain, how are we going to enforce that? What do they define as 'cruising'?" you ask.

"Cruising is defined as any person operating a motor vehicle within a shopping or commercial area without the express intent of using the services of the establishments," the captain replies.

"Pretty vague—how do we know if they're cruising or using the establishments?" you continue.

"I don't know. Use your discretion. I guess let them cruise around the parking lot two or three times without parking, then write them up. Anyway, I want you and your officers to issue warning tickets this month just so the kids will know about the new law," Captain Adams advises.

As instructed, you and your officers wrote a number of warning tickets to the "regulars" over the following three weekends. Unfortunately, the warning tickets did not seem to have any substantial effect on the traffic. When the new law went into effect, you and your officers seemed to write citations pretty much nonstop for the next two weekends. The city judge, upset that he was not consulted about writing the new law and concerned about its constitutionality and vagueness, dismissed all "cruising" citations that came into his court. You too are concerned about the vagueness of the new law and about the police not having input on how the problem might be resolved.

"The city council just passes some law to satisfy a few people and lets the police take the heat," you think to yourself.

As you suspected, problems began cropping up among the teenagers and your officers. Officers, attempting to enforce the new law, were ridiculed by the young people, called names—even spat on. This, in turn, caused your officers to become more hostile and aggressive with the teenagers. Arrests for disorderly conduct, failure to obey lawful orders, and even incidents of assault on officers were increasing. The merchants were also still complaining that the police were not doing a proper job of enforcing the law. Now, parents are complaining that officers have harassed and hassled their children without legal cause. There have been several complaints, some justified, that officers wrote citations to people for cruising when, in fact, they were looking for a place to park in a crowded parking lot. One of your officers, a bit overzealous in his enforcement of the new law, even wrote up an elderly man and his wife for cruising when they went around the parking lot three times looking for a place to park close to a drug store. The teenagers are also blaming the police for enforcing the law, creating even poorer relations among your officers and the people they are supposed to serve.

Your watch commander calls you to headquarters just three weeks after the new law went into effect.

"Jim, the chief is supposed to present reasons why your officers have not enforced this cruising law at the next session of the city council. He called me demanding to know why we're not getting any results. I told him the judge wasn't enforcing the fine, so essentially there were no teeth in the law. He said that's the judge and city council's problem, not ours. Our problem is enforcing the law, not interpreting it. He's got the mayor on his back and numerous complaints from merchants, shoppers, and parents. He told me to come up with something to present to the city council. Now, Jim, you know more about what's going on out there than any of us. So I'm passing the buck on to you. This is your chance to come up with some solution to this problem. You've got three days to give me something I can take to the chief as a possible solution that he can present to city council."

You leave the captain's office despondent. The city council stirred this mess up, created an even greater problem, and *now* they're asking for police input. The merchants want a safe, comfortable shopping area. Shoppers do not want to fight teenage traffic, but the kids have rights too and really nowhere else to go for fun. Unless you can get transferred out of Zone 3, you've got to come up with some workable solution before the situation gets out of hand at the shopping center. What are you going to tell the captain?

Based on what you have read, answer the following questions:

1. List the rights each group has in this case: the merchants, the shoppers, the parents, and the teenagers.

2. What are some of the reasons for teenage cruising? Why are some places more popular than others? What problems exist for the teenagers and the police with cruising?

3. What solutions would you have if you were the sergeant?

RIGHT SIDE OF THE TRACKS— WRONG SIDE OF THE LAW

You are a criminal investigator for a medium-sized sheriff's department serving a county population of nearly one million people. The sheriff, an elected official, usually keeps out of the business of law enforcement and would rather seek public attention and political recognition. The sheriff has indicated that he would like to seek a higher public office such as state representative in the near future. The chief deputy, Hal Owens, takes care of the daily business of running the sheriff's department.

You have received a call from the principal at one of the county's high schools regarding possible drug dealing, vandalism, and larcenies occurring in and around the school. You are scheduled to meet with Mr. Jaynes, the school principal, this morning.

"Good morning, Mr. Jaynes. I'm Detective Bill Anderson," you state as you walk into the principal's office.

"Yes, good morning. May I get you a cup of coffee?" Mr. Jaynes asks as he reaches for the coffee pot.

"That would be great, thanks. I take it black," you respond, sitting down next to the desk.

"I know you're busy so I'll get right to it. We've had some problems with vandalism and larcenies here at the school. I've also been suspicious of some of the students possibly being involved in drug dealing here on school grounds," Mr. Jaynes explains.

"Do you know who they are?" you ask, fumbling for your pen.

"Well, I don't have any proof, but I've made a list of those students I suspect. They hang out together," Mr. Jaynes states, handing you the list.

"I'm not too familiar with these names, except . . . is this Guy Edwards, Jr. the state senator's son?" you ask, pointing to the list.

"Yes, it is. I know you must be surprised because of his father's position, but he's no angel here at the school. Those other kids are all from good families too. Bobby's father is a physician, Andy's is an attorney, and Gary's is president of the oil company here," Mr. Jaynes continues.

"Well, I am surprised these kids would get into anything as serious as drug dealing," you respond.

Later that day you decide to visit the district attorney to determine the best tactic in investigating the case.

"Yes, Bill, I see why you are concerned after reading this list of names," the D.A. states.

"I wanted to check with you to see how I should go about investigating these allegations," you respond.

"I'm not too concerned with the vandalism and petit larcenies at this time, but I am concerned about their involvement in selling drugs. I would suggest you stake out the school where they've been known to deal and get the usual evidence, photographs, and so on," the D.A. states.

Two weeks later, one of your undercover surveillance officers calls you to report that three of the boys had been arrested at the stakeout. One of the boys is the state senator's son, Guy Edwards, Jr.

"Caught them red-handed, Bill. Had 'coke,' 'crack,' and a bunch of Dilaudids they were selling like candy," the detective tells you while handing you the arrest reports.

"This is their first offense according to Juvenile Hall. They'll probably get off with probation and some community service work," you state.

The next day, Chief Deputy Owens calls you into his office.

"Bill, we've got a little problem with these kids on the dope charges. You know one of them is Senator Edwards' son. Senator Edwards and the sheriff are of the same political party and are good friends. The senator has been supporting the sheriff to run for state representative. You also may know that the D.A. is seeking the same office and is in a different party. Now, the D.A. wants to press this for all he can get politically. If he can get some bad publicity for Senator Edwards and the sheriff, it may help him during his campaign. The sheriff wants to know if you can help get these kids off as easy and as quickly as possible without a lot of media attention. Now, I'm not talking about doing something unethical here. If those boys are truly guilty, the sheriff says to throw the book at them. He can't afford a scandal either with something that looks like a cover-up," the chief explains.

"I understand. I'll see what I can do," you reply.

You have a meeting scheduled with Ralph Davis, a juvenile probation officer at Juvenile Hall.

"Ralph, what about these kids? Are they really rotten or do they have some hope?" you ask, referring to the arrest reports.

"I've never seen such a bunch of cry babies in my life. These kids are scared to death. You know, I've been in this business a long time and I know when I'm being conned. These kids have just gotten in with the wrong guy. They've all admitted to dealing drugs for this adult guy named Scooter Johnson, and they said they'd testify against him. All they were looking for was some excitement and I guess some attention," Ralph advises.

"So, they're willing to testify against their supplier, huh?" you acknowledge.

"I'll tell you something, Bill. That D.A. doesn't care about getting Johnson. All he's interested in is convicting these boys. He told me he's going for incarceration for these kids at Afton State Youth Center," Ralph advises.

"The kiddie prison?" you ask in a surprised manner.

"That's right. These kids don't need to go to Afton. I could handle them on probation and you could get their supplier on adult charges. If you will go to the judge with me, I believe we can convince him of that," Ralph explains.

You know that Ralph may be correct in his judgment. The boys would have a better chance on probation than incarcerated. You could satisfy the sheriff and get the adult supplier as well. However, you need a good working relation with the D.A.'s office. The D.A., even if his priorities are different, may be correct in pressing for incarceration. After all, the boys were dealing some hard drugs and may even be involved in other illegal activities. They may have even conned Ralph into believing their story. You remember when you were their age. You came up the hard way with no special privileges. Your father was a steelworker who believed in his country and the law. Besides, you never have cared much for cry babies. Still, this is their first offense, even if it is a rather serious one. What are you going to do?

Based on what you have read, answer the following questions:

1. Should you go along with the juvenile probation officer and recommend probation? Explain the pros and cons of your decision.

2. If the boys were allowed on probation, what might result in terms of the boys' future? What if they were incarcerated?

3. How do you think your decision will affect your relations with the sheriff? The D.A.?

CASE 6
HOMEGROWN TERRORISM

"I don't know why you're hassling us. It's his kind that blew up that plane with real Americans on it! Who knows what he and his friends were planning to do next?" the sixteen-year-old boy protests.

"Yeah, my Daddy says they won't rest until all Americans are dead, and besides, they worship the devil!" his fifteen-year-old sidekick adds.

You look at your patrol partner, Mary Bivins, before responding to the two youths you have just arrested for assault and vandalism. After a deep breath, you return your gaze directly to the youths.

"You two brave patriots beat up a seventy-five-year-old American citizen and tried to burn his house down. Mr. Hafiz and his wife have lived in that neighborhood for the last twenty years. In fact, one of his sons is a police officer over in the twelfth precinct, and he has another son who works as a fireman up in Albany. You two boys are in a whole lot of trouble."

The fifteen-year-old's mother brings coffee into the living room where the two boys, their parents, and the two police officers are sitting.

"How is Mr. Hafiz?" she inquires.

Officer Bivins' response is to the point. "He has a concussion and two broken ribs—"

The sixteen-year-old's father interrupts Officer Bivins impatiently: "C'mon, officers! They were just being rambunctious teenagers who got carried away. I'll make sure they apologize to the Hafiz family, and us and the Ungers will see that their house is repaired. Who knows where kids get the crazy ideas they have these days? They didn't mean no serious harm."

Putting the coffee cup down, you look at the Evans and Unger families.

"I can't say what your sons' intentions were or where they got the idea to do what they did. The fact is, they committed a serious assault and caused extensive property damage. Officer Bivins and I will have to take them to the juvenile detention center. You can try to arrange to have them released to your custody tomorrow until the court hearing."

81

You and your partner ride in silence on the way back from the detention center. Finally Mary speaks: "I can't believe those parents, especially Mr. Evans."

"Yeah," you respond, "I'm not so sure they shouldn't have been arrested as well."

Based on what you have read, answer the following questions:

1. Can parental opinions and prejudice sometimes influence their children to commit acts of violence?

2. Is it difficult to maintain an unbiased perspective and sense of balance when acts of terrorism result in the loss of innocent lives? Should the police and/or the courts take this into consideration under circumstances like the one outlined above?

3. How can schools, police and other social and government institutions educate and help prevent such acts against persons of different ethnic or racial backgrounds?

CASE 7
A LOVING FATHER?

You are a criminal investigator for a small police department serving a city of 78,000 people. You have worked as a criminal investigator for seven of your twelve years in the police department. Although crime in your city is not as serious as it would be in larger cities, you find there is plenty of work to do for a three-man detective division.

June Wilson, an attractive Human Services social worker, has given you a telephone call.

"Pete, we need to get together and talk," June states.

"I'll chat with you anytime, anywhere," you state in a flirting manner.

"Now be nice, Pete. I'm serious. I've got a case you need to be involved in. I've got a 15-year-old girl and her 10-year-old sister in my office and they're accusing their father of rape," June explains.

"Who did he rape, their mother?" you ask.

"Afraid not. He allegedly raped them," June responds.

"I'll be over in a few minutes," you advise.

Walking into June's office you notice the two girls sitting on a couch in the reception area.

Exchanging hellos, June continues, "Hi, Pete. Just got off the phone with the juvenile court judge. She's sending over a court order to place the girls into protective custody at the Emergency Youth Shelter until this investigation is over."

"How did you find out about this rape thing?" you ask.

"The older girl told her school nurse what had happened and the nurse called me. I went over to the school and interviewed the girl briefly. Then we picked up her sister," June explains.

"When did they say their father raped them?" you ask.

"It wasn't a single act. Evidently this has been going on for some time with the older girl, Alice. Alice said her father began having intercourse with her when she was 11. Now she says her father is having intercourse on a regular basis with both her and her 10-year- old sister," June replies.

"This is sick. Do you think they're telling the truth?" you ask.

83

"I've talked with both of them together and separately and I believe they're sincere. We'll have to go through the routine of taking their statements and videotaping their responses," June advises.

"Who's their father?" you ask.

"Name's Freddie Allen, resides at 1010 Elm Street with wife Eleanor," June states, reading from her notes.

"Is that the same Freddie Allen who teaches at the junior high school?"

"One and the same. He also is the choir leader at school, teaches Sunday school, and is the youth advisor at church," June responds.

"I'll need to talk with Mr. and Mrs. Allen," you advise.

"They're on their way here now," June replies.

A few minutes later the Allens arrive at June's office.

"What's going on here? Why are my kids down here?" Mr. Allen questions, angrily pushing his way into June's office, his wife following a few feet behind him.

"Sit down, Mr. Allen, Mrs. Allen. I'm Detective Rogers and this is Ms. Wilson. We need to ask you a few questions," you advise them in a calm, yet assertive voice.

"Look, all I want to know from you is why my kids are here and not in school," Mr. Allen repeats, his wife looking scared behind him.

You notice Mr. Allen is sweating profusely and appears to be on the verge of an emotional outburst.

"Mr. Allen, I must advise you of your constitutional rights . . ." you explain, verbally reading the Miranda warnings from your notebook.

"What's this all about? What am I supposed to have done?" Mr. Allen questions, getting more agitated and red-faced.

"Your daughters have accused you of having sexual intercourse with them on several occasions. A violation of state penal code number 245-23-454b," June explains, reading from her notes.

"Wait a minute. That's a lie. I've never touched them. Ask my wife; she'll tell you I've never touched them. I'll take a lie detector test. Bring them in here and let them say it to my face. They must be on drugs or something," Mr. Allen angrily interjects.

"Mr. Allen, I would suggest you contact your lawyer about this. The judge has issued a court order to place your daughters into protective custody until this is resolved. I personally haven't taken any statements from them yet. I'm not ready to ask you any specific questions until after I've interviewed your daughters," you explain.

"Freddie would never do anything like this. He's a good father and a good husband. He's a good provider. I don't know what we would do without him. My daughters are mistaken," Mrs. Allen adds with a shaky voice.

"I assure you, Mr. Allen, we will get to the bottom of this. We just needed to inform you of the current situation," you advise.

"Where are they? I'll get to the bottom of this. Let me talk with them," Mr. Allen demands.

"I can't let you do that at this time, Mr. Allen. You and your attorney will have a chance to cross-examine them later," you advise.

You proceed to make an appointment for Mr. Allen to come to your office tomorrow and he leaves in a belligerent and frustrated manner. After talking with the two girls you learn that the 15-year-old reported her father because he started having intercourse with her sister. She always felt protective of her younger sister and felt she had to report her father before it was too late. You believe the girls are telling the truth but find there is little physical evidence to back up their story. It is basically their word against the word of their father and mother.

You remember past experiences where juveniles have lied about having sex with adults. Just last year you investigated a coach at the local high school for allegedly having molested some of the cheerleaders. He was acquitted. A terrible joke was played on him by some of the girls, but his career was ruined. No one ever believed he was really innocent after the accusations. You are aware that if the girls are telling the truth, the father is in need of help and might even molest the kids at school, if he hasn't already. You wonder how to best pursue the investigation and where to draw the line between arresting or not arresting.

Based on what you have read, answer the following questions:

1. What are the legal guidelines for gathering evidence in incest and child sexual molestation cases?

2. What are the characteristics of father-daughter incest and child sexual molesters in general?

3. Would you bring charges against Freddie Allen given the evidence at hand? How would you go about gathering evidence in this case?

CASE 8
WELCOME HOME?

You are a state trooper working interstate patrol near a metropolitan city. You are on your way to meet a fellow trooper to run radar for the afternoon traffic.

Just as you pass under a bridge, you see two subjects walking on your side of the interstate. As you look in the rearview mirror, you can tell that the subjects are both female, and one appears to be very young. You decide to turn at the next exit and see if the girls are in need of assistance. Passing the girls on the opposite side of the highway, you notice the oldest girl trying to hitch a ride. You pull across the median strip in order to stop the girls.

The oldest girl appears to be twelve or thirteen years old, while the younger girl appears to be six or seven years old. When you ask the oldest girl to show some identification, she tells you she does not have any. You open the passenger door and ask the girls to sit in the front seat. Both girls appear to be scared, hungry, and tired. They apparently have no baggage, money, or even warm clothing.

You ask the girls where they are going, and they tell you they are looking for food. The oldest girl tells you her name is Lisa and her sister's name is Ann, but she will not tell what their last name is or where they are from. It seems the girls have run away from home. The youngest, Ann, has several small scars on her face. She has remained silent, letting her older sister do all the talking. One of Lisa's arms appears crooked, as though it had been previously broken and had healed without being properly set. Both girls are dirty and seem to be malnourished.

After some coaxing, the two sisters let you take them to a nearby burger joint, where they wolf down the food you order for them. With full stomachs, they seem more comfortable with you. Finally you ask Lisa if she and her sister are afraid to go home, and she tells you they are. In a choked voice, she explains that her parents beat her and Ann frequently, especially Ann. She goes on to tell you that she and her sister have been living in an abandoned warehouse for the last four days.

You call your supervisor on the radio and advise her that you have two juveniles in custody and will not be able to set up radar. You indicate

86

that you are transporting the girls to the county juvenile advocacy center where a social worker can interview them.

When Lisa hears what your intentions are, she grows more fearful and tells you that she has been at the juvenile home before and that, after a short stay, they returned her and her sister to their parents. Lisa requests that you take them home rather than to the juvenile facility, adding that maybe their parents will not be too mad at them. You ask where she lives, and she tells you her home is about ten miles away. Advising headquarters that you are going to the girls' home, you proceed to Lisa's address to get a better assessment of the parents and the situation. Maybe you can do some good.

The parents live in a shabby house out in the country. You decide to talk with them first and leave the girls in your patrol car. Both parents are home watching television, and neither seems concerned that their daughters have been missing for four days. They ask what you want, and you explain to them that you have the girls outside in your cruiser. The mother indicates that she had been wondering when they would get tired of their "shenanigans" and return home. The father is still watching television and does not speak to you. The mother tells you to let the girls come on in and that she will handle them.

Based on what you have read, answer the following questions:

1. What should you do at this point?

2. What other agencies and resources can assist you in this sort of case?

3. The girls' previous experience with juvenile services hasn't been very positive. How might you be able to help remedy that situation?

Section IV

THE POLICE AND THE EMOTIONALLY DISTRESSED

Introduction

Police officers, although they may not always realize it, use psychology daily in their interactions with people in the community. Because police officers deal primarily with people who have problems, they must try to develop and utilize observation and communication skills in order to perform their job effectively and efficiently.

Communications make human interaction possible. The police officer should possess a variety of communication skills when dealing with people in their care. Police officers who are inclined to get involved in altercations and physical confrontations with citizens and suspects need to analyze themselves and may, in some cases, need professional guidance. Exaggerated feelings of insecurity combined with self-doubt about one's own identity as an authority figure can interfere with the process of becoming a professional police officer. Naturally, there are insecure citizens and suspects with poor self-control, which may result in a physical assault against a police officer; this being the case, the officer should contain the individual with a minimum amount of force. As police psychologist Martin Reiser (1973) states, "it is usually easier to talk a suspect into jail than to fight him."

Experienced police officers realize that "explaining things" is neither pampering citizens nor a sign of weakness on their part. It is merely a professional approach to getting the job done in the easiest and least stressful manner.

Verbal communication is not the only form of communication. A police officer may use the correct words, but may employ them in an incorrect or inadequate manner. Being too serious is an occupational hazard for many police officers. It comes, in part, from attempting not to get personally involved in a situation and playing an authoritarian role. Nevertheless, curtness and coldness during communication frequently leads to misunderstanding. A smile or kind word reminds the citizen that a police officer is really a human being and not a rigid authoritarian figure lacking in compassion or understanding.

Police Interaction with the Emotionally Distressed

Dealing with an emotionally distressed individual requires interpersonal skills, patience, and understanding on the part of the police officer. The majority of distressed persons are afraid, withdrawn, passive, and unable to communicate rather than hostile, angry or aggressive.

There are some basic ground rules for police officers handling emotionally distressed or mentally ill persons. First, a police officer should obtain as much background information about the individual and the situation as possible. Talking with witnesses, family, and friends will help provide a more realistic assessment of the situation and avoid unnecessary disruption or danger. Second, when in doubt, police officers should always call for assistance. Assistance may represent security for the emotionally distressed individual and motivate him or her to respond more openly. It is always easier and more professional to call for assistance rather than to resort to fighting with a mentally ill person.

Third, police officers should explain to the individual what they are going to do before they do it. Police officers should not lie to an emotionally or mentally distressed individual, or talk as if the person in distress cannot possibly understand the situation. Police officers should, at least, attempt to communicate with the individual as if they were a relatively rational, normal person. Finally, the police officer should avoid threatening gestures, verbal abuse, or physical force except in extreme cases. Usually, emotionally distressed individuals are compliant and agreeable if they are given assurance that the police officer is a friend who will help rather than threaten the individual's already uncertain stability (Mohandie and Duffy, 1999; Turnbaugh, 1999; Wellborn, 1999).

Mentally unstable individuals such as potential suicides, hostage takers, or snipers are particularly dangerous. A police officer's main concern in such cases should be the safety of others and him- or herself. If the police officer is convinced that prompt action is necessary to protect the interests of the emotionally or mentally distressed individual and others, force may be required.

Zusman (1975) commented that in dealing with mentally ill and dangerous individuals, police officers are in a "damned if you do and damned if you don't" situation. The threat of force or use of force by an emotionally unstable individual is a crime unless there are extenuating circumstances. If police officers attempt to make an arrest and hurt a mentally ill individual, the police are guilty of overreacting and brutality. On the other hand, if the police fail to use force or arrest an emotionally unstable individual, the police are held liable if the individual injures himself or another person (Shah, 1989; Wellborn, 1999).

Police in the Helping Role

There are three recognizable components of the police in the helping role: (1) appeal for help, (2) immediacy, and (3) authority. Police officers are usually the first summoned when a crisis occurs (appeal for help); they have a highly organized mobile response capacity (immediacy); and they have the symbolic and legal power to do something (authority). Police officers constitute an often underutilized resource for the management of unpredictable mental health situations. Police already deliver such service, but in some instances the delivery is grudgingly performed and often inept. The role of the police is explicitly a control function and implicitly one of a helping dimension. Police officers, for a variety of reasons, often emphasize the control function and de-emphasize the helping role. This particular attitude is reflected in the common police expression, "we are police officers, not social workers." Although their role as a helping agent is denied by many police officers, it is this role that has become the predominant one in police work and one that requires the highest degree of skill and competence (Wellborn, 1999).

Since police officers should be especially sensitive to evidence of a crisis in victims of criminal activity, it is suggested that part of the police responsibility at a crime scene should be concerned with the mental health of the victim. The investigating police officer should take a few extra minutes to assess the immediate impact of the encounter upon the victim. Obtaining information necessary to determine if an offense has occurred and, if so, apprehension of the offender should, in a sense, be a secondary concern for the police.

Police officers often have more experience with rape victims and their families than do many mental health professionals. Since most investigating police officers are male, their gender alone may serve as a barrier to open communication unless care is taken to develop an open and receptive atmosphere for the victim (Kerstetter and Van Winkle, 1990; Bachman, 1994). The investigating police officer must proceed with the assumption that each reported rape is genuine (Krahe, 1991).

The range of unpredictable emotional crises that come within the purview of the police seems infinite. The police are positioned in time and place for an array of helping roles that coincide with their role as law enforcers. The immediacy of time and place regarding the police role cannot be achieved by any other group of persons in the helping system. However, this is not to say that the police are obligated to perform a clinical mental health or ministerial function.

Bittner (1967) indicated that in real police work, provisions of the law represent a resource that can be utilized to handle a vast array of problems. There are boundaries in legal guidelines that dictate when illegal offenses have taken place and when police action is necessary. However, these legal guidelines are broad interpretations and do not fit every situation exactly, particularly when police officers deal with the apprehension of mentally distressed individuals. Police officers must rely on informal practices and experience in such cases rather than on strict interpretation of legal guidelines (Gillig, 1990; Turnbaugh, 1999).

There are numerous situations where the police officer is inclined to ignore the behavior of persons who are apparently emotionally distressed or mentally ill. The police frequently receive phone calls from persons who are under delusions that others are trying to harm them. When a serious crime receives publicity, the police are besieged by persons ready to confess; many are known to the police from past experience as relatively harmless individuals. It is a common practice for the police, in order to protect against false confessions, not to release certain information to the press about a serious crime. Although falsely confessing to a crime may constitute interference with the police and an obstruction of justice, criminal proceedings are rarely instituted against these people and, unfortunately, referrals to helping agencies are even more rare.

Police Authority for Handling the Emotionally Distressed

The job of dealing with emotionally distressed individuals is often left to the police. The problem of inadequate medical facilities and helping agencies is indicated by numerous complaints of police officers. Despite the fact that most state laws appear to give police officers adequate legal protection when apprehending persons they reasonably suspect to be dangerously mentally ill and in need of emergency care, the statutes are, at best, complicated and confusing. Many police officers fear the possibility of civil suits for damages and refuse to act unless there is a clear violation of the law. Most police officers, when dealing with emotionally distressed violators, prefer to make an arrest and let other agencies, such as the courts, decide whether to invoke the criminal justice system or provide medical care. This being the case, police officers usually wait until a legal violation occurs before taking action, rather than reporting or acting on obvious emotionally or mentally distressed individuals before a violation occurs (Ruiz, 1993).

While police recognition of persons who are emotionally distressed seems to be a problematic issue, there also seems to be little point in heightening police perception of the emotionally distressed individual unless concomitant measures give police officers some realistic hope of being able to deal with such cases by means other than arrest (Bae, 1981; Ruiz, 1993; Wachholz and Mullaly, 1993; Mohandie and Duffy, 1999).

Summary

Police officers frequently find themselves playing the role of psychologist and mental health counselor. Many police officers do not view intervening with mentally distressed persons as a police duty. Nevertheless, police officers are expected to assist with emotionally distressed individuals because of their potential for violence and their frequent disturbance of social order and peace. Police officers frequently come in contact with individuals who exhibit a wide range of mental and emotional problems. In each case, police officers are expected to make judgments and satisfactorily resolve the problem so that the public's safety as well as the safety of the distressed individual is assured. Such decisions and actions can be difficult and complex tasks, particularly when police officers are expected to resolve the problem successfully without adequate training or benefit of information regarding the individual's mental health history. Because it is difficult for most police officers to recognize mentally distressed and emotionally unbalanced individuals all the time, it is important for them to receive as much training as feasible concerning the handling of emotional problems. Whether the police like it or not, they are the only immediate authority for helping mentally distressed and emotionally unstable individuals.

References

Bachman, R. (1994). *Violence Against Women*. Washington, DC: National Crime Victimization Survey.

Bae, R. P. (1981). "Ineffective Crisis Intervention Techniques: The Case of the Police," *Journal of Crime and Justice*, 4(1).

Bittner, E. (1967). "Police Discretion in Emergency Apprehension of Mentally Ill Persons," *Social Problems*, 15:278.

Gillig, P. (1990). "What Do Police Officers Really Want from the Mental Health System?" *Hospital and Community Psychiatry*, 41(6): 663–665.

Janis, I. (1958). *Psychological Stress: Psychoanalytic and Behavioral Studies of Surgical Patients*. New York: John Wiley & Sons.

Kerstetter, W., and B. Van Winkle. (1990). "Who Decides? A Study of the Complainant's Decision to Prosecute in Rape Cases." *Criminal Justice and Behavior*, 17(3): 268–283.

Krahe, B. (1991). "Police Officers' Definitions of Rape: A Prototype Study," *Journal of Community and Applied Social Psychology*, 1(3): 223–244.

Law Enforcement Study Center. (1970). *Mental Illness and Law Enforcement*. Washington, DC: Washington University Press.

Mohandie, K., and J. E. Duffy. (1999). "Understanding Subjects with Paranoid Schizophrenia." *The FBI Law Enforcement Bulletin*, 68(12): 8.

Reiser, M. (1973). *Practical Psychology for Police Officers*. Springfield, IL: Charles C Thomas.

Ruiz, J. (1993). "An Interactive Analysis Between Uniformed Law Enforcement Officers and the Mentally Ill." *American Journal of Police*, 12(4): 149–177.

Shah, S. (1989). "Mental Disorders and the Criminal Justice System: Some Over Arching Issues." *International Journal of Law and Psychiatry*, 12(2–3): 231–244.

Turnbaugh, D. G. (1999). "Curing Police Problems with the Mentally Ill." *The Police Chief*, 66(2): 52.

Wachholz, S. & Mullaly, R. (1993). "Policing the Deinstitutionalized Mentally Ill: Toward an Understanding of its Function." *Crime, Law & Social Change*, 19(3): 281–300.

Wellborn, J. (1999). "Responding to Individuals with Mental Illness." *The FBI Law Enforcement Bulletin*, 68(11): 6.

Zusman, J. (1975). "Recognition and Management of Psychiatric Emergencies in Emergency Psychiatric Care," in H. Resnick and H. Ruben (eds.), *Emergency Psychiatric Care: The Management of Mental Health Crises*. Bowie, MD: The Charles Press.

CASES INVOLVING THE EMOTIONALLY DISTRESSED

The next eight cases are designed to portray the numerous instances of emotional distress and related problems to which a police officer must respond. Emotional instability does not limit itself to mental illness but may include a wide range of human emotions, which may erupt into any number of unexpected events. The fact that human emotions sometimes result in unexpected behavior is a problem of which the police officer should be aware. Many times police officers have found themselves placed into the role of psychologist and counselor.

In the following cases, you will find yourself facing a variety of human emotions and mental disturbances. How you react in each of these cases will determine whether the emotional disturbance may be of a transient nature or may result in more permanent psychological damage or even physical harm to the individual, the police officer involved, or the community.

Case number one, "A Victim of Rape?" deals with an unsympathetic police officer investigating a possible rape incident. The officer finds difficulty in relating to the victim, suspecting that she has been sexually permissive in the past. The officer finds that his attitude seems to be contributing to the problem of the rape victim.

Case number two, "Police Psychologist," involves two police officers attempting to take a mentally distressed individual into custody. Although the individual has committed no crime, the officers must serve a court order to have the man committed to a mental institution. The technique of "arrest" the officers decide to use may mean the difference between a peaceful arrest or serious injury to the officers or the subject.

Case number three, "I Did It," centers on a police detective who has realized that some mentally distressed individuals confess to crimes they have never committed. In this case, the detective finds himself attempting to prove an individual's innocence rather than guilt.

Case number four, "A Christmas Wish," focuses on a police officer attempting to help a homeless person obtain shelter from the weather. The homeless person refuses the officer's help, and the officer must decide whether to forget trying to help or to force the subject to seek shelter on Christmas Eve.

Case number five, "Prominent Deviance," deals with a police officer who confronts a prominent citizen committing a sexually deviant act with a small boy. The officer must decide on a course of action that will best treat an emotional problem as well as protect the community.

Case number six, "The Chase," examines a common problem among a majority of police departments—how to handle high-speed pursuits of intoxicated drivers. In most instances, the police officer must rely on his or her common sense and discretion. In this case, a police officer involved in a high-speed chase with an intoxicated driver must decide if chasing the driver is the correct way of handling the problem.

Case number seven, "No Job and No Hope," portrays a police officer who is faced with a highly emotional individual threatening to commit suicide. Among a large crowd of bystanders, the officer must attempt to talk with the individual and persuade him not to kill himself. Although the officer is faced with many types of approaches to use and much advice from fellow officers and the growing crowd, he finds it is up to him to decide.

In Case number eight, "Suicide by Cop," A Hispanic Internal Affairs Investigator has to investigate a white police officer who shot a young African-American male who ran toward him, pointing a pistol which turned out to be a toy gun. Apparently the victim was suffering from chronic depression. The challenge concerns turning in a report and recommendation to your captain that is both racially sensitive and fair to the victim, his family, and the officer in question.

CASE 1
A VICTIM OF RAPE?

You are responding to a sexual assault call. The report is from an apartment complex in a poor section of the city. The only information you were given is an apartment number, which was relayed to the dispatcher by a neighbor of the victim.

As you approach the entrance to the apartment, a woman swings the door open and says, "It's about time you showed up."

You recognize the woman as Janice, a prostitute who works the neighborhood. Jokingly, you ask if she has been raped. Janice sneers at you and says no. Leading you inside the apartment she introduces you to a young lady sitting on a couch, crying. "She's the one that was raped." Janice says to you. You ask her if the young lady is a friend and she tells you that she is. You also ask Janice if the young lady is a prostitute. Janice indignantly responds that the girl is not a prostitute.

The young lady is dressed in a short, see-through nightgown. She does not appear to be injured physically. The apartment does not appear to reflect any recent violent actions. You begin to wonder if Janice is telling the truth about the girl not being a prostitute. You see no evidence of a husband or children living in the apartment with the girl. You have worked in this neighborhood for quite a while and have begun to realize how young girls living alone in apartment buildings like this one make their living—as prostitutes.

"What's your name?" you ask the girl. "Ann . . ." the girl answers as she looks up at you and wipes the tears from her face.

You ask Ann if she knows her assailant and she gives you a description, indicating that she knows his first name. "Pete, that's the only name I know him by," she explains.

"Then you do know him?" you ask with some degree of skepticism.

"He's just an acquaintance," Ann snaps back.

You are now becoming more convinced that Ann is a prostitute and Pete was probably a nonpaying customer.

"Did Pete rape you here?" you ask while looking around the apartment.

"In the bedroom," Ann responds.

"Naturally," you think to yourself as you survey the bedroom.

"What do you do for a living?" you ask Ann.

Ann explains that she just moved to the city a few weeks ago and is looking for a secretarial position.

"Well, Ann, to be completely honest, this doesn't look good," you explain. "First, you say you're raped by some guy that you are acquainted with and only know that his name is Pete. Second, your apartment doesn't appear to have been broken into by force. Third, you don't have any bruises or cuts on your body that would indicate a man assaulted you."

"Well, what the hell would you do if a guy has a damned knife at your throat?" Ann shouts at you angrily.

You try to keep your composure as you say, "I don't mean to be an asshole about this, but if I went out and arrested this Pete guy, it would only hurt you. A trial jury would laugh you out of the courtroom. The jury would have you pegged as a prostitute by the time the defense attorney was through with you."

You continue by pointing out to Ann that it would probably be a waste of time if she went to the hospital for a checkup in that all the reports and procedures that would have to be done would more than likely be thrown out of court.

Ann begins to cry again and tells you to forget the whole matter.

Walking out the door, you turn and tell Janice to be sure that her new apprentice gets the payment in advance the next time. She responds with a glare.

Two days later at roll call your sergeant makes an announcement. "Men, we've apparently got a rapist on the loose in the northeast section of the city. All we know is that he tells his victims his name is Pete. This guy raped a minister's wife last night and the boss wants us to catch him before the media come down on us."

As the sergeant describes Pete and the M.O. he uses, you remember the rape call you investigated two days ago. The description and the M.O. match the statement Ann had made to you. You are now faced with forgetting about the incident with Ann or returning to her apartment to obtain a statement. You realize you probably made a mistake treating Ann's rape as lightly as you did. If you go back now, she will probably be uncooperative, and your supervisor will want to know why you didn't complete the investigation in the first place.

Based on what you have read, answer the following questions:

1. Describe yourself as portrayed in this case in terms of your own statements and thoughts.

2. What can you do at this point? List all the options and describe the probable consequences of each.

3. What does your own state law say about the evidence required for rape (i.e., force used, resistance by the victim, etc.)?

CASE 2
POLICE PSYCHOLOGIST

"He's in here, Officer. I can't do a thing with him."

A frail, elderly lady leads you and your partner down a hall and points to one of the bedrooms.

The document in your back pocket is a commitment order signed by a doctor and the judge instructing you to take a young man into custody for mental treatment.

"I just can't handle him anymore by myself. He's just gotten worse since his father died," the woman explains to you as she opens the bedroom door.

As the door swings open you see Bobby sitting in the middle of the floor. The room is a mess with broken furniture, clothing, and papers scattered over the floor.

"Is he violent?" you ask the woman.

"He does get upset sometimes and throws things; I'm scared of him," the old lady dejectedly replies.

Bobby is sitting on the floor with his feet pulled up close to his body and his eyes fixed on the wall in front of him. Bobby is about six feet tall and weighs close to 200 pounds.

"Let's not get him mad at us," you whisper to your partner.

Your partner walks into the room next to Bobby and kneels down beside him. "Hi Bobby, how are you feeling today?"

Bobby doesn't respond and continues to stare at the wall in front of him.

"Would you like to go for a ride with us? We'd like to drive you to see a friend of ours."

Bobby begins to rock and his eyes widen, still staring at the wall.

"Do you need some help getting up?" Brian asks, attempting to get a grip around Bobby's arm.

"No!" Bobby screams as he lashes out with his arm and strikes Brian across the face.

The blow knocks Brian off balance from his kneeling position. Brian is now sitting on the floor rubbing his head.

Bobby runs to a corner of the room and sits down, holding his legs up around him.

You enter the room quickly and kneel down next to Brian.

"You OK?"

"Yeah, I guess so," your partner replies.

"Please don't hurt him," the old lady says as she pleads with you and Brian to be careful.

You know from past experiences that if you try to take Bobby by force and he gets angry, he will be afraid of anyone in a uniform. As a result it will be harder to handle him in the future for police or healthcare personnel.

You survey the bedroom and notice there are two large windows. The bedroom is on the first floor of the house and it would not be difficult for Bobby to jump through a window and escape.

Brian is getting impatient and says, "C'mon, let's get the cuffs on him."

After several more moments of deliberation you agree with your partner. "Alright, but let's make sure he doesn't go out the window," you explain while getting your handcuffs ready.

Walking toward the corner where Bobby is seated, you tell Brian to hold Bobby's legs and feet while you get the handcuffs on his wrists.

"Be sure to pull him out and turn him over on his belly so I can get to his arms," you explain to Brian.

Bobby's eyes begin to widen again as you and Brian start toward him.

Brian jumps at Bobby's feet and tries to get a grip around his legs. Bobby begins to scream and starts kicking with his legs. You try to grab Bobby's arms to turn him over. Bobby uses his leg to strike Brian in the stomach, causing Brian to release his hold. Bobby jerks away from your grasp and retreats back into his corner.

"You OK?" you ask Brian, frustration written all over your face.

"Yeah. But this is getting ridiculous. Let's not baby him anymore or one of us is really going to get hurt. We're going to have to choke him down," Brian states as he pulls his baton from his belt.

"No, please don't hurt him. He doesn't know what he's doing. He's never hurt anyone before," the old lady begs, running over to Bobby and holding him.

"Look, lady, we've got no choice," Brian tells the woman.

Brian seems to be right, but you are not sure. You feel sorry for Bobby and his mother, but things are getting out of hand. Something has to be done.

Based on what you have read, answer the following questions:

1. What should you and your partner do?

2. What would be the probable consequences to Bobby's physical and mental health if you used force? Do you think the force used may be injurious to psychological treatments for Bobby?

3. Bobby appears to trust his mother. Can she help in any way? Explain.

CASE 3
"I DID IT"

When you joined the police department four years ago, you realized that you would come in contact with many different types of people. You have become concerned that most of the individuals with whom you came in contact regarding police problems are either poor or have emotional problems. Your concern was increased when you were promoted to the criminal investigations bureau. You rarely arrest or convict anyone who is wealthy or anyone involved in "white-collar" crimes. Those individuals are generally investigated by state or federal agencies and not by the local police force.

As a police officer, you have seen poorer people and emotionally distressed individuals receive poor treatment and punishment that people with wealth and power never seem to receive. As a result, you have tried to treat everyone as equally and fairly as you can.

You have been working the Crimes Against People unit of the detective division for two months. During that period you have investigated several rapes and numerous robberies and assaults. You have recently been assigned to investigate a series of rapes that have occurred at the city's university.

The city university is a resident four-year college with less than 10,000 students. There is a small security force that patrols the campus, but it has neither the human resources nor the facilities to investigate major criminal acts such as rape. You have been assigned to work with the campus security force in the current investigation involving four rapes that occurred on campus during the past three weeks. All of the rapes have been at night, and all but one have been outside the dormitories. The attacker apparently selects girls who are walking alone from a night class back to their dormitory and assaults them under cover of the many shrubs that surround the dormitories. The one inside assault was committed in the laundry room of one of the dormitories late at night.

The description of the attacker is sketchy, but all the girls agree that the man is white, 20–25 years old, five feet nine to six feet tall, and smells like a mechanic. The girl who was attacked in the laundry room only caught a glimpse of the man before he placed a pillow case over her head. You have been concentrating your investigation around the many service stations in the area in order to locate a suspect.

The girls on campus are living in fear and are beginning to carry hammers, knives, and even firearms with them. The campus police have been giving lectures about rape prevention in the girls' dormitories but have not been very effective in reducing the fear. The university administration and the news media are demanding that the suspect be apprehended. There is even pressure from the police administration to make an arrest as soon as possible.

One morning as you sip a cup of coffee and review some of the statements of witnesses you have been interviewing, you receive a telephone call from campus security.

"Allen, this is Jeff from the campus police. I believe we've got the rapist; you want to come down and talk to him?" You respond affirmatively and gulp down the last of your coffee. Leaving the office, you hope that this is not just a false alarm.

Driving to the campus you think how great it would be for you and everyone concerned if the suspect was the rapist. You have been hassled by several police administrative officers to get the case cleared. The newspapers have been calling you every day wanting to know what progress has been made in apprehending the rapist, and you feel relieved to be able to have something to report when they call today.

Walking into the campus police office, you meet Jeff, one of the security officers, waiting for you with a grin on his face.

"Craziest thing I've ever seen. This guy just came in early this morning and confessed to all the rapes. Said he wanted to get it off his chest," Jeff says enthusiastically.

"Let's make sure we don't violate any of his rights or mess this thing up," you warn.

"Hell, he just came in and said he did it. One of those spontaneous confessions. Didn't want a lawyer or anything. Already got his statement," Jeff proudly announces.

Walking into the small conference room you see the suspect sitting in a chair, looking out the one window in the room.

"You a detective?" the young man asks as he turns to you.

"My name's Allen Osborne. I'm with the city police. What's your name?"

"David Farrows," the young man answers as he pulls a pack of cigarettes from his pocket.

You notice the suspect's fingernails as he lights a cigarette. His fingernails have black grease under them as if he had been working on an automobile engine. "You a mechanic?" you ask Farrows, remembering that the rape victims all smelled the odor of gasoline on their assailant.

"Yeah, I tinker around with cars a little. I got a part-time job at the race track helping out."

"Were you advised of your rights by the campus police?" you ask, worried that the investigation may be thrown out on a technicality.

"Yeah, I signed one of them waiver forms. I don't need no lawyer. I just want to get this over with. I already gave a statement to the campus cops."

Jeff hands you the waiver of rights form and a handwritten statement.

"Did you write out this statement yourself?" you ask David.

"Yeah, might have some misspelled words in it, but I never was no good in English."

You read over the statement and find it to be somewhat sketchy. There is little detail about how the suspect actually committed the rapes. The statement reflects everything the newspapers have carried about the rape accounts. You ask David about the fine details of the rapes and he becomes angry.

"Look, I did it and I confessed to it, so let's get it over with. Take me to jail!"

"Has the suspect got a record of sex offenses?" you ask Jeff.

"Sure does; nothing like this, but he's been busted for indecent exposure and voyeurism on campus," Jeff explains while looking down at a clipboard.

You pull out the case file from your briefcase, including the evidence list. There is little physical evidence to associate anyone with anything. There is no stained clothing, no semen samples from the hospital, and no blood samples. The rape victims either took a bath after the rapes or the doctors could find no external semen samples. You look over the newspaper accounts and compare them with David's statement.

"Damned newspapers have to print everything and make it harder to do a good investigation," you mutter to yourself, noting the similarities between the newspaper stories and Farrows' statement.

One thing the newspapers did not describe was the knife the assailant used.

"Did the suspect have a knife on him?" you ask.

"Yep, right here," Jeff acknowledges as he empties a property envelope and pulls out a folding hunting knife.

The type of knife used in the rapes was a folding hunting knife that is very common. You think to yourself how coincidental and circumstantial this evidence is. Pushing aside any doubts you might have, you thank Jeff and carry the suspect down to headquarters for booking.

Several days later the campus police send you a report in which several witnesses observed the suspect on campus during the times of the rapes. You also know that the rape victim who was in the laundry room positively identified David as her assailant in a lineup.

After reading the report you are still unsure of the suspect's guilt. All the evidence is circumstantial, corroborated by one girl's identification of David and the description of the knife. It is enough evidence for a conviction, especially since the suspect admits to committing the rapes. But somehow you are still doubting David's guilt. The fact that he is unable to give a detailed account of the rapes and appears to enjoy the attention he is receiving has led you to believe that he is not the rapist.

Your superiors have not supported your beliefs about the suspect's innocence. They appear to be more concerned that an arrest has been made and the media are off their backs. The administration has ordered you to close the case and to begin work on other pressing investigations.

The fact that there have been no rapes or sexual assaults on campus since the suspect was placed in custody does not relieve you. Especially since a young man was arrested on campus the previous evening for stealing gas from parked vehicles. Has the real assailant been appre-hended or is it just a matter of time before another attack occurs? What are you going to do?

Based on what you have read, answer the following questions:

1. List the evidence against the suspect. List your reasons for not believing the suspect is indeed the offender. What defenses would the suspect have in court?

2. Do you have any options to pursue the investigation longer?

3. How do the news media affect police investigations for better or worse?

CASE 4
A CHRISTMAS WISH

You are a young police officer in a midsize city. It is Christmas Eve and you have just finished your shift. It began raining late in the afternoon and, with the exception of some last-minute shoppers, things were pretty uneventful. The cold rain began to change to ice when you got off at eight. You are on your way home to be with your family when you see a homeless woman struggling with a cardboard box near an alleyway. You shake your head and find yourself feeling sorry for the woman. She appears to be about the same age as your mother. You know your spouse and son are expecting you home, but you don't want to leave this woman out in the cold rain. All she has to protect her from the cold is the cardboard box. After some thought, you turn your patrol car around to see if you can help.

When you walk up to the woman's box, she starts yelling at you.

"Get away . . . leave me alone. Why don't you chase criminals or something instead of bothering me? I've not done anything."

You explain that you are just trying to help and ask if she would get into the patrol car so you can talk with her. She begins screaming at you again.

"You're not taking me to jail. I haven't done anything. Don't bother me. Leave me be!"

You become frustrated. Here you are, standing outside in the cold rain trying to help someone who does not want your help. As you are being screamed at by the woman, you begin to think about your spouse and son waiting for you at home. You even begin to wonder if you did the right thing in stopping.

"Why am I doing this?" you ask yourself. "I need to get home and put my son's bike together. He'll be going to bed soon, and I want to get a chance to play with him a while before he's off to bed."

You decide that you cannot leave the woman out in the icy cold. You get into your patrol car and ask the dispatcher to contact the shelter to see if they can take the woman. As you are waiting for the dispatcher to call you back, you notice that the woman's cardboard box will not hold up much longer in the rain. You know you must do something and wish you could make her understand that you just want to help.

"Unit 27, the shelter says they are full but they may be able to make room for her. You'll have to transport, though. By the way, the weather information says it's going to be in the low teens tomorrow and below zero tonight with the windchill around minus fifteen degrees," the dispatcher says.

As you get out of your car, the wind hits your face and already feels much colder than it was before. You approach the woman, and she begins to yell at you again.

"Why can't you cops leave me alone? No wonder people call you pigs."

"Look, lady, I am trying to help you. If you don't come with me to the shelter you'll probably freeze to death out here," you respond, trying to convince her.

The woman begins to curse you and spit at you. You realize she will never go to the shelter voluntarily.

"OK, lady, have it your way. Stay out here and freeze if you want to. I don't need this abuse. Have a very merry Christmas," you say with disgust as you walk away.

As you leave, you advise the dispatcher that the woman will not go to the shelter with you. You also ask the dispatcher to make sure the next shift patrol in this zone checks on her. As you hang up the microphone, you know the next shift will probably not have time to check on the woman. After all, it is Christmas Eve and, with a skeleton force working the next shift, they'll probably have their hands full answering other calls.

The time you spend at home allows you to forget about the woman. Your spouse kept dinner warm for you, and your son was eager for you to come home. He was so excited about Christmas. As you put him to bed, he said his prayers and asked that everyone in the family be together, safe and warm on Christmas. Your son's prayers make you think about the woman you left out on the street. You can hear the wind howling outside. You wonder what she is doing.

Based on what you have read, answer the following questions:

1. Is it uncommon for homeless people to refuse help? Why would this woman refuse to be helped on such a cold, rainy night?

2. Should you return and attempt to help the woman or force her to seek shelter? Do you (as the police) have the legal authority to force someone to seek shelter? If the woman froze to death, would there be any liability on your part?

3. Assume that the next patrol shift cannot check on the woman. What would you do?

CASE 5
PROMINENT DEVIANCE

You are a police patrolman assigned to a walking beat near a city park. It is early spring and the favorable weather has increased the number of persons visiting the park. On weekends the park is almost overrun with small children and teenagers. Since you have to work the 3 to 11 P.M. shift, you must handle all the minor problems associated with young people in the park. Lost children, injuries, teenagers necking, and occasionally alcohol and drug problems arise that you must try to resolve. Your town is small and fortunately does not have the major problems associated with big cities.

One evening, just as the sun is setting, a young girl in her early teens comes running up to you while you are making your rounds. She is obviously upset.

"Officer, I need to talk to you."

"What can I do for you?" you ask, smiling at the girl.

"A man tried to attack my little brother in the rest room at the park," the girl exclaims, her voice shaking.

The girl leads you into the park where her little brother and an older boy are sitting on a bench. The girl introduces you to her brother and her boyfriend.

"This is Adam, my brother, and Jackie, my boyfriend."

"What happened, son?" you ask.

Adam doesn't appear as upset as his sister.

"Nothing, really. I went in the rest room over there and a man was inside. He wanted to touch me and offered me money," Adam tells you while pointing toward the park's public rest room.

"What did you do, Adam?"

"I ran. I was kind of scared of him."

You determine from Adam's remarks that the incident happened about twenty minutes ago. Adam tells you that he never saw the man before and didn't know him. The older boy tells you that he and his girlfriend were sitting on a park bench talking when Adam ran up to them.

"Me and Susie were sitting over there when her brother came running up to us and told us what happened. I ran over to the rest room to see if the man was still there and he was gone. Then Susie saw you and decided she'd better report it.

"How old are you, Adam?" you ask, taking out your notebook.

"Eleven next month."

"Can you describe the man in the rest room?"

"He was old, about forty and big and fat. He had on a dark suit, black hair and was bald on top," Adam explains.

"Would you recognize him again if you saw him?" you ask Adam.

"Sure would!" Adam exclaims.

You obtain full names, addresses, and other information for your report from the children and tell Adam to advise you if he ever sees the man again. You spend the rest of the shift walking around the park area looking for a possible suspect.

At the end of the shift you give the motor patrol officers on the relief shift a description of what happened in the park.

"Hey, I had a similar report like that last month," one of the relief officers remarked. "This woman complained that a man tried to pick up her little boy in the park rest room. In fact, it was on the 3–11 shift before I rotated to graveyard."

"Did you file a report?" you ask the officer.

"No, I didn't think it was important at the time. You know how upset mothers get if somebody looks cross-eyed at their kids. Besides, the kid didn't appear too upset about it. However, he did give a description that matches the one you have of the man."

You arrive at work a little earlier the next day so you can check with the records and complaints bureau about similar reports in the park. You find two complaints of attempted sexual molestation of young boys in the park from last summer. The description of the man that Adam gave closely resembles that of the suspects in the complaints.

You decide to watch the rest room in the park closely to see if anyone matching the description appears. As darkness grows near you reason that it might be a good idea to go inside the rest room and wait for awhile. The rest room is empty, and you look for a stall in which you can wait undetected.

After thirty minutes of waiting and watching people come and go, you begin to feel somewhat like a deviant yourself.

"If somebody sees me in here, they might assume I'm a sex deviant," you think to yourself.

Just as you decide it's time to leave and make your rounds, two young boys enter the rest room. The boys are about ten to twelve years old and appear to have been playing baseball. Within a few seconds, another individual enters the rest room, and from your stall you can only see the man's back. You carefully open the stall door in order to observe more clearly. The man matches the description from the reports. He is a big man dressed in a suit. You are unable to see the man's face from your vantage point. The man approaches the two boys. "Hello boys, what are your names?" the man asks.

"I'm Timmy and this is Giles," one of the boys answers.

"How would you two boys like to make ten dollars apiece?" the man asks as he takes out his wallet.

"What do we have to do?" one of the boys replies somewhat suspiciously.

"Just something that will make us both feel good," he explains in a soft tone, as he begins to hold and fondle one of the startled boys.

Leaving your stall, you state, "Mister, I want a word with you. I am a police officer."

Turning toward you, the man's eyes are wide with fear. You recognize his face immediately. He is Charles Tussell, a prominent citizen in the community. Tussell is a member of the school board as well as several community organizations, and an alderman on the city council. He is also president of a bank in your city.

"Why, Mr. Tussell, what are you doing here?" you ask in a surprised manner.

"I, uh . . . I uh . . . just came to . . . uh . . . wash my hands, officer." Tussell answers, perspiring heavily.

After obtaining the names and addresses of the two boys, you advise them to wait outside for you. You know that you have seen and heard enough to convince you that Tussell is the sex deviant you have been looking for, but the two boys will have to make a statement.

"Mr. Tussell, I want to inform you of your rights . . ."

"Please officer, I . . . uh . . . I can't afford any bad publicity. I have a wife and two daughters. Please let me go. I'm receiving professional help from Dr. Anders in Bakerville. You can check with him. Please!"

You ponder the situation. You have heard of Dr. Anders, a psychiatrist in the neighboring town of Bakerville. Tussell is very embarrassed and scared. He may be telling the truth, or he may be lying just to get you to let him go. No one has been physically hurt by Tussell's propositions, but then again, there is no way to measure the emotional damage that may have been caused by his behavior. If you make an arrest it could cause a lot of complications in your town. If you let Tussell go, he could continue his sexual deviance somewhere else, or he could continue to receive treatment for his problem. Your gut reaction is to "throw the book" at him. Yet, you want to use your mind as well as your emotions to do what is most appropriate.

Based on what you have read, answer the following questions:

1. What should you do?

2. If Tussell is arrested and brought up on charges of sexually molesting children, what do you think his penalty would be?

3. Can Tussell's problem be treated or should he be placed in a penal institution?

CASE 6
THE CHASE

You are sitting in your cruiser, parked near an intersection on the outskirts of the city. It is two o'clock in the morning and you are thinking how much you would like to be asleep. The midnight shifts seem to get longer each night. Suddenly, a car speeds through the intersection, running a red light. You blink and watch the car for a second, thinking to yourself that the driver must be doing at least eighty miles per hour. You pull out of your parking place and begin pursuing the speeding automobile. You call headquarters and inform them that you are running one south on Papertree Road. As you start to gain on the car, you look at your speedometer, which now reads 90 miles per hour. Getting close to the car, you reach forward and turn the spotlight on the speeding car. The driver begins to brake and pull off to the side of the road. As you pull in behind the car, you try to note the license plate, but it is covered with mud and is difficult to read. You call headquarters again and inform them that you have stopped the car and are going to check the driver.

You step out of your cruiser and begin to walk toward the car. Just as you approach the driver's window, the car suddenly jumps into gear and speeds off. You go back to your cruiser and resume pursuing the offender. You are becoming angry. The driver is now driving erratically, as though he or she were intoxicated. You call headquarters again and advise them of what happened, adding that you may need some backup intercepting the car. The dispatcher informs you that one backup car is heading toward your area.

The offender you are chasing is driving more and more recklessly. The car has already exceeded 100 miles per hour and almost crashed into a delivery truck. The car heads toward the interstate entrance ramp, running another driver off the road. You have just pulled behind the offender and are beginning to wonder where your backup car is. You also begin to wonder if you are doing the right thing in chasing the car. The car is going over 115 miles per hour and almost wrecked two other vehicles, which could have resulted in the death or injury of innocent people, not to mention placing you in jeopardy. If you stop chasing the car, the driver may slow down and go home without incident. On the other hand, the driver may not only be intoxicated but a wanted felon as well.

The car has just run another car off the interstate and into the median strip. Your backup car has not arrived. What are you going to do?

Based on what you have read, answer the following questions:

1. List the options you have at this point. Which option seems to be the best? Explain.

2. If the backup car had arrived at this point, would it change the situation?

3. What policies would you make as a chief of police for similar encounters and situations?

CASE 7
NO JOB AND NO HOPE

You are responding to a suicide threat. The call came from a subdivision on your beat. The subdivision is next to the city limits and is composed of middle-class residents. As you approach the neighborhood you realize that you will be the first officer to arrive on the scene. The backup units will have to fight the lunch-hour traffic as they respond from further away in the city.

As you approach the area, you notice a group of people gathered in a field across the main street that services the neighborhood.

"Must be where it's happening," you think aloud to yourself.

You see an open gate and dirt road leading into the field and pull into it. Driving closer to the group of people, you recognize what they are looking at—a large electrical cable support tower. There is a man halfway up the tower, on a service ladder.

"That tower must be at least 200 feet high," you mutter to yourself.

You have never worked a suicide attempt before and certainly never a "jumper." The thought of someone jumping from a high structure in order to end their life is upsetting to you.

Walking up toward the crowd you see several individuals you know who live in the subdivision.

"Who is that on the tower?" you ask one of the men standing in the crowd.

"Bert Jacobsen. He's threatening to jump but won't do it," the man responds.

"Why does he want to jump?" you ask.

"Who knows, the guy's crazy."

You recognize Bert as a resident of the subdivision. You have never had any police dealings with Bert but have stopped to chat with him on occasion. Bert always likes to work in his yard, trimming, planting shrubs and flowers. That is how you met him. During the spring and summer you would see Bert working in his yard and you would pull up to the house and talk with him about gardening. You never realized that Bert had the kind of emotional problems that would lead to a suicide attempt.

The sound of sirens breaks your train of thought. Two more police vehicles and an ambulance have arrived. One of the police vehicles is carrying your shift lieutenant.

"What have you got?" the lieutenant asks. You quickly respond, "The guy's name is Bert Jacobsen. I just got here myself. I don't know what his problem is."

The lieutenant begins to talk with the members in the crowd, attempting to find out why Bert is threatening suicide.

Walking up to you, the lieutenant tells you what he has found out: "Apparently, this fellow got laid off six weeks ago when the aerospace industry cut 2,500 jobs, and things kind-of went from bad to worse. Do you know where this Jacobsen fellow lives?"

"524 Houston Place," you answer.

You continue to tell the lieutenant that you believe Bert has a wife and a couple of children but that you have never met them. The lieutenant motions for one of the other police officers to come over to where you are standing.

"Will, go over to 524 Houston Place and see if the guy's family is over there. His name is Bert Jacobsen."

"How well do you know this guy?" the lieutenant asks you.

"He's just an acquaintance. I've talked with him before, just chit-chat," you explain.

The crowd of people is growing, and some of the members are yelling for Bert to jump.

"That's all these people want to see. They want him to jump and then they'll blame us for not doing anything," the lieutenant states in an aggravated manner.

The lieutenant orders another police officer to try to disperse the crowd or at least to keep them quiet.

"I figured it wouldn't take long for them to get here," the lieutenant gestures toward a local TV van and newspaper reporter entering the field. "You say you've talked with him before. You're probably the best one to try to talk him out of jumping," the lieutenant advises you.

Will comes back from Bert's house and advises the lieutenant that there is no one home and no one in the neighborhood apparently knows where Bert's family is.

A television camera crew and newspaper reporter and photographer begin walking toward you and the lieutenant.

"We had better figure out what we are going to do before they start making a big deal of this," the lieutenant advises you.

The lieutenant decides that you should go to your patrol car and use the P.A. speaker to talk to Bert.

"Ask him to come down and talk with us," the lieutenant continues.

You run over to your patrol car as the TV and newspaper reporters gather around the lieutenant. You begin to think how impersonal everyone is acting toward the situation. Several younger members of the crowd are shouting at Bert to jump, and the ambulance team looks like a bunch of vultures waiting to scrape up the remains. You pick up the microphone and speak to Bert.

"Bert. Bert, this is Jim Wade with the police department. I'd like to talk to you. I'd like to help you. I'm going to come up to where you are and talk with you."

Bert makes no movement from his perch on the ladder. He is over halfway up the tower with his arms wrapped around the ladder, holding his head down against his right arm.

You begin to walk toward the tower and the lieutenant stops you.

"I didn't mean for you to go up there and talk to him. It's too dangerous."

"I believe I can talk to him more effectively if I go to him," you explain.

"All right, but be careful. If he is going to jump, don't let him take you with him," the lieutenant warns.

"Use reverse psychology on him. Tell him to go ahead and jump and he won't do it," a fellow officer advises you as you approach the tower.

"Tell him anything he wants to hear," another officer advises.

As you start up the ladder, you realize it will be you alone who has to talk with Bert. Although you aren't sure what the nature of Bert's problem is, you feel pretty certain that it has something to do with his layoff. Whatever the problem, you must try to solve it perched 100 feet above the ground. You have never liked heights much, but you know you have to try.

Based on what you have read, answer the following questions:

1. Are you doing the right thing in going up to see Bert?

2. Assuming that you are successful in getting close to Bert, what should you say and/or do?

3. Is the crowd creating a confusing situation for Bert? How would you deal with the crowd and the press?

CASE 8
SUICIDE BY COP

What a mess! You can't believe your bad luck in being chosen for your current assignment. You have been working in Internal Affairs for five years and have never seen a situation like this. You can still hear Captain Johnson's words ringing in your ears.

"Gonzalez, you must not be living right. You've got a doozy of a case," he had said, handing the file to you. "Be careful."

Now after conducting a thorough investigation, it's six weeks later and time to forward your recommendation to the captain.

A young African-American male, 21 years of age, got into an altercation with a white police officer doing a foot patrol in a predominantly black neighborhood. The young man ran toward Officer Jerry Simmons, also 21, pointing a pistol at him in broad daylight. Officer Simmons had very little time to react. He drew his weapon and shouted for the young man to halt. When the man failed to stop, Officer Simmons fired his pistol three times, fatally wounding the man in question, who died on the way to the hospital. It turned out that the gun was a toy replica.

Initially, the media reported the incident as another instance of racism and police brutality, which was supported by several bystanders who witnessed the incident. Your investigation has turned up disturbing evidence. Apparently the shooting victim, Anthony Deakins, suffered from chronic depression and had told several family members and acquaintances that he had figured out a way to end his suffering. Since for the last several days before he was shot he had seemed much happier, friends and family had ignored what he had said. You have concluded that in all likelihood, Anthony had gotten a police officer to do what he couldn't bring himself to do. Still, your chief has made it clear that he is sensitive to public opinion, and there are some in the community who demand that Officer Simmons be punished. What they didn't know was that Jerry Simmons himself has been experiencing depression and had been under treatment by a departmental psychologist prior to the shooting incident. It seems he has had a great deal of trouble with the fact that he had shot an unarmed man.

The district attorney has publicly stated that the grand jury will be examining the case and that your report will be included in the presentment. You know your report will have a significant impact on what the grand jury decides to do.

Your report is due tomorrow. You know the chief will want you to consider the community's concerns, and you also want to be sensitive to the victim's family. You regard Officer Simmons as a victim as well.

Based on what you have read, answer the following questions:

1. What are some potential problems that could arise if the community feels the shooting incident is swept under the rug? What do you think the grand jury would do?

2. How could the incident be reported to the media and public in a way that would be sensitive to both the victim's family and Officer Simmons?

3. How might this event affect Officer Simmons personally and professionally?

Section V

POLICE STRESS

Introduction

Police officers are the subject of continual scrutiny by the people they serve. They are routinely faced with complicated and frequently dangerous problems in which they are supposed to react quickly and, at the same time, correctly. As police psychologist Martin Reiser (1970) points out:

> The police officer is in the middle of forces pushing for social changes on the one hand and forces which want to severely punish anyone who deviates from society's norms on the other.

The police officer finds him- or herself often locked into a "no-win" position—there will always be someone to voice disapproval of police behaviors.

Police departments are typically organized in an authoritarian, quasi-military fashion. This organizational structure of the police profession has been adopted by virtually every police department in the United States. The military model was designed so that people within the system could efficiently receive and respond to orders issued by superiors. Soldiers, especially in the lower ranks, are not expected to make complicated decisions—only to respond to orders. Police officers, however, are constantly expected to make decisions and solve complicated problems (Swanson, Territo, and Taylor, 1997).

The police officer occupies a difficult role. He or she must be effective interpersonally but usually has little or no training for such skills. The police organization often fails to reinforce improvement in police officers' use of crisis counseling and human-relations skills. The officer must always try to maintain control of situations which he or she may misinterpret—yet, at the same time, must avoid conflict. The officer also finds it necessary to adapt to an occupation in which one moment may bring a threat of death while other extended periods of time may be boring and routine. The police professional must attempt to be an effective decision maker and an independent problem solver within a system that encourages dependency by its very structure (Stevens, 1999; Roberg, Crank, and Kuykendall, 2000). The result of such occupational paradoxes is currently referred to as "police stress."

Police Stress as an Occupational Hazard

Several studies of health and safety among occupational groups have identified the police profession as having a high incidence of stress, due to police social components. Crank and Caldero (1991) found that police officers adapt to their occupational situations. The psychological makeup of the police officer develops from a sociological framework of the police profession. Many new police officers lose the friends they had as civilians and develop friendships with other police officers during this adaptation period. Individuals who have no prior history of stress-related diseases or accidents prior to becoming police officers, in some instances, develop these diseases and accident-prone characteristics after employment as police officers (Stevens, 1999). The period of time during which police officers seem to go through the most stress is when the new officer begins to acquire police personality traits. This adaptation period frequently leads new officers into stress-related characteristics such as divorce, increased smoking habits, increased use of alcohol and drugs, heart disease, and accidents (Reviere and Young, 1994). A second adaptation period seems to develop after police officers retire or resign from the profession. After adapting to the stress of police work, officers who leave the profession must readjust to the general social environment, which frequently leads to a high incidence of alcoholism and, in some instances, suicide (Arrigo and Garsky, 2002).

The concept of police stress seems to have formally evolved in 1974 when Kroes, Margolis, and Hurrell researched the police profession to determine the effects of job stress on the health of police officers. Kroes, Margolis, and Hurrell found that, as an occupational group, the police profession was the second most stressful occupation in the United States (air-traffic controllers were first). Kroes, Margolis, and Hurrell identified different types of stressors the police frequently encountered including court schedules, shift work, administrative frustrations, community relations, poor equipment, and role ambiguity. In addition, the fear of civil litigation is often cited as a major cause of stress. The next two decades depicted a proliferation of lawsuits against the police, ranging from improper use of force and false arrest to failure to provide appropriate protection and services.

All police officers are subject to police stress, but many officers are capable of handling stressors in a variety of ways and in varying amounts depending upon their own personal capabilities and the particular police environment in which they work. Attempts have been made to identify the potential for stress in individual police officers and the police environment (Crank, Regoli, and Hewitt, 1993; Stevens, 1999). Police officer characteristics which have been identified as "stress indicators" include divorce, cigarette smoking, alcohol and drug use, headache frequency, high blood pressure, and stomach ailments. Police environment characteristics which have been identified as "stress indicators" include size of the police department, administrative support, regulations, salary ranges, employment duties, number of hours worked, and shift rotation schedules (Patterson, 1997).

Stress and the Police Family

The family members of the law enforcement officer often find themselves in a unique and frustrating position. Other non-law enforcement families may view them with some degree of suspicion and distrust because of the police occupation. This can create a potential for the family to become alienated and isolated from the rest of the community, which, of course, can have a devastating impact on relationships within the family as well. If the family is isolated, family members may break down into separate and sometimes antagonistic relationships. In some instances the parents may join together and exclude the children. Sometimes the mother forms a relationship with one or more of the children and excludes the father. The excluded father may form a closed relationship with a favorite daughter or with someone outside the family (Braswell and Meeks, 1982).

It seems apparent that family communication is particularly important for the law enforcement officer, since they often find themselves in a social vacuum with their primary and sometimes only friends being fellow officers and their families. The family is, perhaps, the most continuous intimate communication environment available to an individual. The criminal justice professional brings his or her work experiences home, whether they are talked about or not, and carries his or her home experiences into the work environment. As a result, open and healthy family communication is a vital contribution to and reflection of the police officer's level of effective communication and human relation skills while at work (Greene, 1997).

The excessive job pressures a police officer may experience trying to maintain control of a variety of situations and to make complicated decisions, can drain his or her energies, leaving the officer depleted and unable to cope with minor or major family problems. The police officer's family, who need and expect some time and attention themselves, are often confronted with a person who simply lacks the emotional resources to deal with his or her family problems. Regardless of whether the problem is large and important or small and trivial, an emotionally depleted police officer will be unable to deal with it (Ryan, 1997).

A police career is more than just an occupation for an individual; it is a way of life for the officer and his or her family. Police marriages are susceptible to stresses inherent in the police profession. Changing work schedules, pressures on the job, long hours, and the threat of danger are but a few factors that can drive a wedge between a police officer and his or her spouse. Greene (1997) notes that police officers have one of the highest divorce rates in the United States.

Stress and the Police Image

One major stress area involves how one defines the role of the police officer in today's society. The police profession includes substantial contradictions and inconsistencies. The duties of a police officer depend upon such factors as the oath of office, statutes of law, court decisions, departmental policies, politics, community pressure, informal quota systems, common sense, and the personalities of superiors. Police officers who patrol the streets find that legalistic solutions to human problems are often inappropriate or unjust, and commonsense solutions are frequently second-guessed (Bayley and Bittner, 1999).

The role conflict and ambiguity inherent in the police profession are multiplied by distorted media images of the police officer. The media often create a fictionalized image of police work that promotes unreal expectations in both citizens and new police recruits. Many young police officers like to identify with the "macho" image of the media's representation of police work. The public and the police alike are constantly being bombarded with the tough, aggressive cop; an image which is in contrast with the helpful, friendly, professional police officer that modern training academies and criminal justice academic programs are trying to graduate today (Crank, 1998).

The nature of police work requires officers to face situations in which they are likely to experience frustration and anxiety during interactions with people. Police officers are expected to deal with serious matters among people who possess a lifestyle different from their own. They may experience culture shock when they move from one subculture to another and may find it difficult to interpret accurately, to predict, or to influence the behavior of those around them (Strecher, 2002). Such discomfort and social confusion often leads the police officer to develop negative attitudes toward those individuals who are different.

Many officers experience trauma after being involved in highly emotional situations. Some officers find it difficult to cope with certain instances of social injustice, injuries, and deaths. Often police officers become deeply and personally involved in certain cases involving victims, injustices, public apathy, and shooting situations (Dumont, 1999). The officer, however, is expected by the public and by his or her peers to approach such situations in an objective and professional manner. The result is the repression of his or her emotions in order to maintain a professional image.

The police officer is trained to display a certain image and to react with authority to given situations. This image is not only provided by the media's representation and public expectations, but by the training academy as well (Violanti, 1993). Police officers are trained to be somewhat suspicious and to perceive events or changes in the physical environment that indicate a probability of disorder (Skolnick, 1994; Kraska and Kappeler, 1997). Training movies depict police officers injured or killed in any number of situations that other individuals would consider normal. Many "shoot–don't shoot" films portray police officers encountering young children, elderly individuals, beautiful women, and other persons unexpectedly bearing weapons. Such training is intended to "alert" the police officer to his or her vulnerability as a target of assault and to prompt preventive measures. Such training may create substantial stress for a police officer, possibly to the extent that the officer may be unable to relate with people who are not police officers as meaningfully as he or she would like.

Coping with Stress

There have been many suggestions for reducing stress or learning to cope with stress in the police profession (Fulton, 1999). Among the most notable suggestions are:

1. More efficient pre-employment screening to weed out those who cannot cope with a high-stress job.

2. Increased practical training for police personnel on stress, including the simulation of high-stress situations.

3. Training programs for spouses so that they may better understand potential problems.

4. Group discussions where officers and perhaps their spouses can ventilate and share their feelings about the job.

5. A more supportive attitude by police executives toward the stress-related problems of patrol officers.

6. A mandatory alcoholic rehabilitation program.

7. Immediate consultation with officers involved in traumatic events such as justifiable homicides.

8. Complete false arrest and liability insurance to relieve the officer of having to second-guess his decisions.

9. The provision of departmental psychological services to employees and their families.

More specific programs designed to increase effectiveness in coping with police stress have included:

1. The enhancement of self-awareness and self-esteem. The individual police officer can often decrease the impact of stress by increasing his/her understanding of the problems they face in police work.

2. Physical exercise and diet. Activities such as aerobic exercise, jogging, swimming, tennis, and similar activities allow a means of ventilation for built-up stress. Diet is another important contribution to the physical well-being of police officers who find themselves under shift changes and long hours, which often has the officer eating nutritionally deficient food (McArdle, Katch, and Katch, 1986).

3. Biofeedback and relaxation training. Instructing police officers in how to relax and control their physiological responses has been successful in many stress management programs.

4. Psychological services and counseling programs. Police officers know what the stresses of police work are but either cannot or are reluctant to talk about them with anyone other than fellow police officers. By training selected police officers in counseling and psychological techniques under the supervision of a clinical mental health professional, police agencies have reported successes in reducing stress-related symptoms in police officers such as alcoholism, drug abuse, and marital problems (Territo and Vetter, 1981; Murphy and Schoenborn, 1987; Moriarty and Field, 1990).

Summary

The police profession has been identified as having a high incidence of stress and stress-related diseases. The causes of stress within the police profession are numerous, but are usually related to the social and political environment in which police officers find themselves working and living. Stress in police work has been demonstrated by relatively high rates of divorce, alcoholism, drug abuse, heart disease, and accident proneness. Police officers are trained to be suspicious of potentially dangerous individuals. Unfortunately, almost everyone a police officer comes in contact with is potentially dangerous. Maintaining a suspicious attitude of others creates a substantial amount of stress in the police officer. Consequently, it could be suggested that police training provides an atmosphere conducive to stress. Several police agencies have developed programs designed to provide ventilation and resolution of police stress for officers and their families. Many police agencies have incorporated counselors, chaplains, ride-along programs for spouses, and auxiliary police services for officers and their families. Many of these programs appear to help relieve the stresses of police work, but much more needs to be done before the police profession can clearly resolve the problem of police stress.

References

Arrigo, B., and K. Garsky. (2002). "Police Suicides: A Glimpse Behind the Badge." In R. Dunham and G. Alpert (eds.), *Critical Issues in Policing: Contemporary Readings*, 4th ed. Prospect Heights, IL: Waveland Press.

Bayley, D., and E. Bittner. (1999). "Learning the Skills of Policing." In L. Gaines and G. Cordner (eds.), *Policing Perspectives: An Anthology*. Los Angeles: Roxbury Publishing Co.

Braswell, M., and R. Meeks. (1982). "The Police Officer as a Marriage and Family Therapist: A Discussion of Some Issues," *Family Therapy*, 9(2).

Crank, J. (1998). *Understanding Police Culture*. Cincinnati: Anderson.

Crank, J., and M. Caldero. (1991). "The Production of Occupational Stress Among Police Officers: A Survey of Eight Municipal Police Organizations in Illinois." *Journal of Criminal Justice*, 19(4): 339–350.

Crank, J., Regoli, B., and Hewitt, J. (1993). "An Assessment of Work Stress among Police Executives." *Journal of Criminal Justice*, 21(4): 313–314.

Dumont, L. (1999). "Recognizing and Surviving Post Shooting Trauma." *Law and Order*, 47(4): 93–98.

Fulton, R. (1999). "Managing Stress Before It Manages You." *Law Enforcement Technology*, 26(5): 78.

Greene, L. (1997). "Uplifting Resilient Police Families." *The Police Chief* (October), pp. 70–72.

Haar, R., and M. Morash. (1999). "Gender, Race, and Strategies for Coping with Occupational Stress in Policing." *Justice Quarterly*, 16(2): 303–336.

Keller, P. (1978). "A Psychological View of the Police Officer Paradox," *Police Chief*, 45.

Kraska, P., and V. Kappeler. (1997). "Militarizing American Police: The Rise and Normalization of Paramilitary Units." *Social Problems*, 44(1): 101–117.

Kroes, W. H. (1985). *Society's Victim—The Police, An Analysis of Job Stress in Policing*, 2d ed. Springfield, IL: Charles C Thomas.

McArdle, W., F. Katch, and V. Katch. (1996). *Exercise Physiology: Energy, Nutrition and Human performance*, 4th ed. Philadelphia: Lea & Febiger.

Patterson, M. (1997). "Shift Your Approach to Handle Those Varied Work Schedules." *Police*, 21(12): 36–37.

Reiser, M. (1970). "A Psychologist's View of the Badge," *Police Chief*, 38.

Reviere, R., and Young, V. (1994). "Mortality of Police Officers: Comparison by Length of Time on the Force." *American Journal of Police*, 13(1): 51–64.

Roberg, R., J. Crank, and J. Kuykendall. (2000). *Police and Society*, 2d ed. Los Angeles: Roxbury Publishing Co.

Ryan, A. (1997). "Afterburn: The Victimization of Police Families." *The Police Chief* (October), pp. 63–68.

Skolnick, J. (1994). *Justice without Trial: Law Enforcement in a Democratic Society*, 3d ed. New York: Wiley.

Stevens, D. (1999). "Police Officer Stress." *Law and Order*, 47(9): 77–81.

Strecher, V. (1999). "People Who Don't Even Know You." In V. Kappeler (ed.), *The Police and Society*, 2d ed. Prospect Heights, IL: Waveland Press.

Swanson, C., Territo, L., and Taylor, R. (1997). *Police Administration*, 4th ed. New York: Macmillan Publishing Co.

Violanti, J. (1993). "What Does High Stress Police Training Teach Recruits? An Analysis of Coping." *Journal of Criminal Justice*, 21(4): 411–417.

CASES INVOLVING POLICE STRESS

Police officers have a tremendous responsibility regarding the maintenance of the social order. Police officers must act in an authoritative capacity, represent the law at all times, be compassionate in some situations and prepared to take a life in others, help remove a lifeless body from a highway and, within the same hour, bear the tragic news to an unsuspecting widow. He or she must witness countless injustices and yet is expected to lead a normal life. It is not surprising that those persons in the police profession often experience high divorce, suicide, accident, and alcoholism rates. Many police officers will face and make more crucial decisions in an eight-hour shift than many nonpolice persons will make during the course of an entire year. One of the keys in becoming a successful police officer is learning to cope with the varieties of stress that the position inherently involves.

As you react to the following eight cases, make an attempt to identify with and to place in perspective the personality characteristics portrayed.

Case number one, "Decisions," concerns a police officer who is faced with two situations at the same time. The officer must make an on-the-spot decision as to which deserves his attention first. The officer finds that sometimes the first decision may not always be the best. There is little time for deliberation in an emergency, and there is no room for error.

Case number two, "Eviction Notice," deals with a police officer forced to serve an eviction order on an elderly couple. The couple has nowhere to go and no one to turn to for help. The officer must do his duty and evict the couple regardless of his emotional feelings about the situation. The officer finds that what is legal is not necessarily just.

Case number three, "A Trained Machine," involves an internal affairs investigation into a police shooting incident. An officer has shot an innocent person by mistake. Some feel the officer should be punished for negligence. It is the officer's fault—or is it?

Case number four, "Family or Job?", deals with one of the more common police stressors—how to be a career police officer and have a stable family life at the same time. A police officer sees his family pulling apart from him and friends making inappropriate demands on his limited free time. Although the officer is happy with his job, can he find a way to prevent his family from breaking up because of it?

Case number five, "Civil Liability," explores the popularity of civil suits against police actions. Police effectiveness is sometimes marred by the always present threat of a civil suit. A police officer must decide if the fear of litigation will impede his performance as an officer of the law.

Case number six, "The School of Hard Knocks," explores the role of a police officer who has been assigned to a high school that has been traumatized by a school shooting, leaving a teacher dead and two other students wounded and one of the assailants committing suicide. The officer in question has been asked by the guidance counselor to come up with a plan to help the students, staff, and parents recover from the tragedy. Although a plan sorely needs to be developed, unfortunately no special training has been provided for the new assignment and fellow officers are less than enthusiastic regarding what needs to be done.

Case number seven, "To Protect and Serve," explores the social isolation police have with the community. A rookie police officer finds that former "close friends" are now becoming more distant and are treating him differently because he is now a police officer.

Case number eight, "Off Duty or Off Limits?", concerns an off-duty officer who is drawn into an uncomfortable situation while drinking in a neighborhood bar whose owner, a former cop who treats his police-officer patrons well, needs assistance with some unruly customers.

CASE 1
DECISIONS

It's your first day back on the 7 A.M. to 3 P.M. shift. You are in the roll-call room of the state police barracks waiting for your sergeant to address the shift before you go on patrol. Sipping a cup of coffee and trying to wake up, you wonder what the weather will be like.

"Hope it doesn't rain. There will be a lot of traffic accidents to work if it rains," you think to yourself.

The sergeant, looking a little sleepy himself, enters the roll-call room.

"All right, men, I don't have any new items for you, but I do want to remind you about the mental patient who escaped from custody yesterday. The city and county have not had any luck locating him, and they have asked us to keep an eye on the interstates. He may be trying to get home. Remember, he can be dangerous. For those of you who have been off for a couple of days, I have some copies of this guy's description and background. Pick one up before you go out. Any questions?"

The room is quiet for a few seconds. When you realize that no one else is going to say anything you raise your hand.

"Sergeant, have you heard what the weather's going to be like today?"

"Oh yes, it's supposed to rain, so be sure you all have enough accident forms," he warns.

After picking up a copy of the escaped mental patient report and checking out your patrol car, you proceed toward your patrol zone. Your patrol zone consists of approximately fifty miles of interstate and nearly one hundred square miles of suburban area near a metropolitan city.

Traffic accidents keep you busy during the first few hours of the shift. Your sergeant was right about the rain. It began raining just after you left the state police barracks and, needless to say, has contributed to a number of commuter accidents in your zone. It is now 11 A.M., and you decide to eat an early lunch and work on some reports at a nearby truck stop. As you start to obtain clearance on the radio, the dispatcher provides new information on the escaped mental patient.

"All units prepare to copy. Be advised that city P.D. has informed us that a homicide has occurred in Fairbanks subdivision last evening. Suspect is described as being the escaped mental patient from the state hospital. Suspect last seen in the Fairbanks subdivision running from the scene in a northerly direction at about 7 A.M. this date. Consider suspect armed with a knife and dangerous."

The report surprises you. You didn't realize that the escaped mental patient was that dangerous. You fumble through your attaché case and pull out the report on the mental patient. After a closer reading, the report indicates that the individual is criminally insane and extremely dangerous. You now wish that you had read the report in more detail, since Fairbanks subdivision is only a few miles from your patrol zone. You decide to telephone headquarters at the truck stop in an effort to acquire more information on the fugitive.

The records clerk at headquarters advises you that the mental patient stabbed an elderly woman to death last night. The patient had broken into a residence at Fairbanks subdivision where the elderly woman lived alone with her two small dogs. The records clerk also informs you that the mental patient stabbed the dogs to death.

Hanging up the telephone you decide to skip lunch in favor of some peanut butter crackers and a soft drink. You feel that you should spend the time patrolling the areas near Fairbanks subdivision looking for the mental patient.

It is still raining hard, and you hope that there will not be any more traffic accidents to work before you get off duty. The radio dispatcher interrupts your thoughts.

"Attention all units in zone 26 and vicinity. An armed robbery has just occurred at the Pike Street Liquor Store. Two suspects seen heading north in a 1991 gray Buick Century. City police were in pursuit of suspect vehicle until lost near Interstate 26 and the Brookcastle Highway."

Zone 26 is your zone, and you're only a few miles from the Brookcastle exit. You begin to head south on I-26, watching the northbound traffic for the gray Buick.

You observe a man hitchhiking on the northbound side of the interstate. The man is dressed in only a shirt and pants, and you think about why the man isn't under a bridge for cover from the rain. You realize that the man could fit the description of the escaped mental patient. As you look for a level area in the median strip to turn you notice a blue Nissan Sentra—with what appears to be two girls— stopping to pick up the hitchhiker. Just as you begin to pull into the median strip a gray Buick speeds by on the northbound side of the interstate. It is raining hard, and you are unable to make out the occupants of the car or its license plate. Pulling onto the northbound lane you realize that you must make a decision. The hitchhiker who was just picked up by the girls may or may not be the patient. The gray Buick could be the robbers or just someone driving too fast in the rain. You have enough probable cause to stop either the Buick or the Nissan.

Making a radio call for assistance would result in at least a five- or ten-minute delay for a backup unit. By that time the vehicle you decide not to stop would probably be lost. You cannot waste any more time. You have to act now.

Based on what you have read, answer the following questions:
1. What should you do?
2. If, in fact, there were no police units close to your location, would your decision change?
3. What probable cause exists for pursuing the gray Buick? For pursuing the Nissan?

CASE 2
EVICTION NOTICE

You have just finished working the morning school traffic at a county elementary school. Looking at the pile of court process papers laying in the seat of your cruiser, you realize that today is going to be a very busy one. Fumbling through the papers to separate the subpoenas and warrants, you find one eviction order.

"Never had to serve one of these before," you think to yourself as you read the order.

The eviction order states that you are to remove two individuals, Mr. and Mrs. Enoch Hall, and their belongings from a rented house. The order further states that Mr. and Mrs. Hall have not paid their rent in over two months and the landlord is attempting to find "relief" from the courts.

"Probably a couple of welfare bums who are too sorry to pay their rent," you think to yourself.

You decide to stop at the landlord's home and talk to him about the eviction. The landlord lives only a few miles from where the Halls' house is located.

"Good morning, Mr. Hughes, I'm Deputy White with the sheriff's department. I understand you have a problem with your renters."

"Did you get an eviction notice to serve?" Hughes asks.

You show Mr. Hughes the order and again ask what the problem is.

"The problem is they won't pay their rent. They've been living there for I don't know how long. I inherited the place from my uncle, who died last year. I'm going to rent the place to some more responsible people," Hughes explains to you.

"When's the last time they paid their rent?" you ask.

"Oh, they pay a little here and a little there. I can't keep track of it. I raised their rent last year hoping they would move, but they didn't," Hughes states.

"How much is their rent?" you ask, somewhat curious about the situation.

"I charge 'em $300 a month. They were paying $175 when my uncle owned the place. They should've moved when I upped the rent. They're on a fixed income," Hughes continues.

From the conversation with Mr. Hughes you begin to realize that the Halls must be an elderly couple. It seems obvious that Mr. Hughes just wants the Halls off the property.

"Mr. Hughes, I don't know too much about civil law, but can you evict a renter if they indicated good faith in paying the rent? You indicated that they have paid some on their rent."

"Look officer, that order has been signed by the judge. I went up to the courthouse and talked with him myself. Known him a long time. We go fishing together. If you've got a question about it why don't you call him?" Hughes responds, somewhat irritated.

Remembering what your academy instructor advised about not getting involved in civil actions causes you to stop questioning the rationale of the order. Your job is to serve court processes and not question whether they are just. You advise Mr. Hughes that you will serve the eviction order and leave.

Arriving at the Halls' home, you notice that the house is a small frame structure.

"It sure isn't worth $300 a month," you think to yourself as you pull into the driveway.

Mr. Hall comes to the door just as you step on the porch of the house.

He is a small, frail man who appears to be in his seventies.

"Mr. Hall, I'm Deputy White with the sheriff's department. I'm afraid I have some bad news for you."

"Morning officer, would you like to come in?" Mr. Hall asks as he opens the screen door.

The inside of the house is what you expected. There are a few furnishings and the living room is dark. You sit down on an old, worn-out couch. Mrs. Hall comes into the living room and asks if you would like a cup of coffee. Declining the coffee and being as courteous as you can, you explain the eviction order to them.

Mr. and Mrs. Hall do not appear surprised about the order.

"Figured he'd get around to throwing us out," Mr. Hall remarks.

"Have you folks paid anything on your rent to Mr. Hughes?" you ask, still concerned about Mr. Hughes's motives.

"Yeah, we've been paying $175 a month for five years now. Mr. Hughes took this place about six months ago and came by and told us we'd have to start paying $300 a month or get out. We're on a fixed income, social security. We've been trying to pay Mr. Hughes on time but sometimes we have to pay two or three payments a month rather than the whole $300 at one time. The wife's been sick, and Medicare doesn't pay all the doctor and drug bills, so we have to pay some," Mr. Hall explains.

"Then you have paid some on your rent and you're not trying to get out of paying?" you ask.

"I'll pay Mr. Hughes what he wants, but I can't pay the whole $300 at one time," Mr. Hall continues.

It is apparent to you that Mr. Hughes is only concerned with making the Halls leave. Hughes either lied to the judge about the Halls not paying their rent or the judge is just a good friend of Hughes and is "helping him out."

"You know, Mr. Hall, I believe you'd have a good case against Hughes in a civil court," you suggest.

"Too much time, trouble, and money. Besides, if Mr. Hughes wants us to get out, there ain't no way to stop him," Mr. Hall states.

"Where are you going to go?" you ask, wondering if the Halls have any children.

"Don't know. Don't have any children that could take us in. I guess we'll just have to find somewhere else to live. Don't have any money. Maybe the county poorhouse will take us," Mr. Hall says with a small grin.

The situation sickens you. You know there must be some underlying motive as to why Hughes wants to evict the Halls. You could call the state department of human services and talk with them about the situation; but you're not supposed to get involved in civil matters. You are a law enforcement officer, not a social worker. Still, it doesn't seem right.

Based on what you have read, answer the following questions:

1. Should law enforcement officers become involved in civil matters?
2. What legal grounds, if any, do the Halls have? What can they do about the situation?
3. What should you do in this case? Are there any resources or institutions available that could aid the Halls?

CASE 3
A TRAINED MACHINE

Female police officers are looked upon with curiosity, humor, and sometimes contempt. As a female investigator in the internal affairs bureau, you occasionally feel that other officers view you with more than the usual amount of contempt. Traditionally, internal affairs officers have been feared by other police officers, and traditionally internal affairs officers have been men.

You have been educated and trained to perform as a law enforcement officer in your city. You have never been assigned to work any "real" police functions during the three years you have been on the force. You were first assigned to the identifications bureau where you worked as a crime scene technician for two and a half years. Desiring to become involved in criminal investigation work, you took and passed the detective exam. Evidently, the administration felt you were more suited to work internal affairs investigations than criminal investigations.

You are getting bored with having to perform background investigations on police applicants and have been requesting more important assignments from your lieutenant. Your lieutenant, a sexist, has promised to give you the next important case that comes along.

A telephone call at 3 A.M. from your lieutenant has just made that promise a reality.

"June, you awake? Listen, you've been wanting a good assignment and I've got one for you. A patrolman shot and killed an unarmed man a couple of hours ago, and we need a case report on it. Get down to headquarters and get on it. The patrolman's name is Frank Schmidt. We're going to see how good a job you do."

You have finally gotten that one important case. Regardless of how distasteful the situation is, you are excited about being assigned as the investigating officer.

Arriving at your office, you find that Officer Schmidt and his sergeant, Joe Banks, are waiting for you. Schmidt is a young officer, probably in his mid-twenties. He is pale and appears to be very scared. Sergeant Banks is chewing a cigar and looking at you with no small amount of animosity.

You introduce yourself and ask Officer Schmidt and Sergeant Banks into the internal affairs conference room.

"I understand there's been a shooting," you say, attempting to hide your nervousness.

"Look, the kid blew away this bastard out behind an all-night market that was robbed. The bastard made a sudden move and Schmidt shot him. The kid did all right," the sergeant retorted.

"Thank you, Sergeant, but I need a statement from Officer Schmidt himself," you advise, noticing that Sergeant Banks is impatiently rolling his cigar from one corner of his mouth to the other.

"Now, Officer Schmidt . . . Frank, tell me as completely as you can what happened."

"Well, I was patrolling the Baker Section when I got this silent alarm call at the all-night market on Duke Street. It was about 1 A.M. and I was only a couple of blocks away, so I got there in a few minutes. As I approached the market, I cut my lights and engine and coasted to the rear of the market. That's when I saw the guy come running out of the market with a bag. The guy ran around to the back of the market and I hollered for him to stop. He turned real fast and looked like he was grabbing something inside his jacket, and that's when I shot three times and I guess I hit him all three times."

"OK, Frank. Did the man you shot rob the store?"

"No, the store clerk said the guy was a frequent shoplifter and he wanted us to catch him this time, so he turned on the alarm. That clerk's not supposed to use the alarm unless it's an armed robbery attempt. He shouldn't have turned on the alarm."

Officer Schmidt is obviously upset. You notice that he is beginning to perspire and is rubbing his hands together nervously.

"Frank, did the man you shot have a firearm or any other type of weapon on him?"

"No, not even a pocket knife," Schmidt replied.

After three hours of questioning Officer Schmidt and obtaining additional details about the shooting incident, you excuse Schmidt and his sergeant.

"OK, Frank, you can go home now. I'll have to obtain statements from some other people; then I'll get back in touch with you. Sergeant, remember that Officer Schmidt will be assigned to day shift in the records bureau until this is cleared up."

Assignment to desk duty in the records bureau is standard procedure for officers in your department who have been involved in a shooting incident. The assignment is supposed to be a "cooling off" period for the officer but in some cases seems to create more stress as the officer waits to see if his or her career will be ended.

After reviewing the statements and circumstances surrounding the incident, you decide with some reluctance that the shooting was unjustified. Newspaper, radio, and television accounts of the incident have also ruled the shooting unjustified and are calling for the prosecution of Officer Schmidt.

Several days later Sergeant Banks enters your office while you are writing your final report to the review board.

"Well, what's going to be in your report to the review board?" Sergeant Banks demands, chewing on what appears to be the same cigar he had three days ago.

"I'm recommending that disciplinary action be taken against Officer Schmidt for unjustified shooting," you answer, not looking up from your typewriter.

"What do you mean? That kid did exactly what he's been trained to do. He got an armed-robbery-in-progress call, got to the scene and saw a man running from the store. He told him to halt, but the man wheeled around and grabbed at something in his jacket. What the hell would you do?" Sergeant Banks yells, getting angrier by the moment.

"He should have made sure the man was pulling a gun," you answer, trying to maintain your calm.

"By that time it could've been too late. Schmidt could be lying in a grave right now, like a lot of other young cops who waited to make sure," the sergeant states as he storms out of your office.

You begin to think about Sergeant Banks' statement. You remember that you have never been on patrol or had to face any of the situations line officers must face in their day-to-day activities. You also remember the training that you received on the use of deadly force at the police academy three years ago. You remember all the training movies and how you joked with other members in the classroom about how hard it was to differentiate a shooting situation from a non-shooting situation.

You begin to think about Officer Schmidt and what your report may do to his life and career. The review board relies heavily upon the internal affairs investigation report for making their decisions. Looking down at the report still in the typewriter, you wonder if you are doing the right thing.

Based on what you have read, answer the following questions:

1. Why would the lieutenant give this case to you rather than an experienced investigator?

2. Do you think police firearms training tends to make officers paranoid?

3. What would you do in this situation? What would you place in the report if you were the investigator?

CASE 4
FAMILY OR JOB?

It's 9 P.M. and you are on your way home from police headquarters. After working twelve hours on a burglary detail, you are bone tired. As a detective working in the property crimes unit of the Criminal Investigation Division for the past seven weeks, you have been involved in a sting investigation attempting to break a burglary ring that has been operating in your city. You enjoy your work, especially since you were transferred from Traffic Division to C.I.D. nine months ago. There seem to be more excitement and more reward for you in investigative work.

Pulling into your driveway, you notice that the family car is gone. "They must have gone out to eat," you think to yourself as you rummage through your pockets for the house key.

Entering the house, you notice dishes in the kitchen sink. Suddenly, you remember that your nine-year-old son is participating in a school play. There's a P.T.A. meeting and school play scheduled for tonight. You were supposed to go with your family but somehow it slipped your mind. You even forgot to call and inform your wife that you would be late getting home tonight.

"Damn," you think, remembering how important your attending the play was to your son.

It is too late for you to go to the school now. The meeting and play are supposed to be over at 9:30. You open a soft drink, sit down in a living room chair, and begin to think about how you are going to apologize to your son.

Working investigations seems to take much more of your time than when you were in Traffic Division. Your schedule in the Traffic Division was more structured. You worked eight hours and came home, the same thing every day. But you were not happy in the Traffic Division. You are very happy in investigations because you are actually doing something that you feel is important. You are making major arrests and getting "real" criminals rather than traffic offenders; nevertheless, you realize that your new position has been hard on your wife and son.

A couple of weeks ago you had to stay out overnight on a surveillance. It just happened that the night was your 10th wedding anniversary.

You remember how understanding your wife was. Sure, she was hurt and disappointed, but she seemed to realize how important this case was to you—especially since you have been working so hard, over sixty hours a week for the past seven or eight weeks. You chuckle to yourself, thinking of your work as work. It is more fun than work, and you are getting something accomplished that is worthwhile.

You hear the family car entering the driveway and you go to the door to greet your wife and son.

"Sorry, this case is really big. We've got thirty or so people we can get closed indictments on already. But we're going to get to the big ones at the top of this ring." You stop short, noticing that your wife does not seem to be very interested in hearing about the case.

"Hi Daddy, how come you didn't come to my play?" your son asks.

"Sorry Billy, but I had to work late. How was your play?" you ask, kneeling down to him.

"You always have to work late," Billy says sadly, walking away.

"Honey, just as soon as this case is over, I'll make it up to you and Billy. I promise," you explain to your wife.

"As I recall, that's what you said during your last big investigation, and then this one came up. For the past nine months it's been one big investigation after another. Billy and I are both getting a little sick of it. Apparently you would rather be at work than here with us," your wife states, almost in tears.

You walk away, not wanting to get into an argument. Your wife is upset now and you decide to let her "cool off." Maybe you can talk to her tomorrow.

The ringing of the telephone awakens you at 6:30 the next morning.

"Hey, it's time to get up. Remember you've got to get down here to relieve Martin at the surveillance site."

The voice at the other end of the line is your partner, Dave. You remember that you asked him to call you this morning to make sure you were awake. You are supposed to relieve Detective Martin, who has been on surveillance all night. You decide not to wake your wife and go into the kitchen to make some instant coffee.

"I'm going to try and take off early today," you say to yourself, realizing you should spend some time with your son and maybe even take your wife out to dinner.

Later that day you ask your partner if he will cover for you so you can take the afternoon off. Dave agrees to the arrangement, and you go home at 2 o'clock that afternoon.

Your wife and son are not home. Billy must be at school and your wife is probably out shopping. You change into some comfortable clothes and gaze out the window. "Lawn needs cutting. I'll cut it this weekend if I have a chance," you mumble to yourself.

The telephone starts to ring and you think about not answering but then decide to answer, since it could be something important about the case you are investigating. The call is not about your case but is from one of your friends.

"Hey, I caught you home. Remember you were supposed to help me get that gun permit this week."

Your friend, Andy, works in a jewelry store in town and wants you to help him obtain a concealed weapons permit. Andy must carry large sums of money and expensive jewelry from time to time and is worried about getting robbed. You told him you would help him obtain the permit. Andy gives you a good discount on the items he carries in his store because you are a friend. With some reluctance, you tell him that you will be over shortly to pick him up and take him downtown to obtain the permit.

Arriving back several hours later, you notice that the family car is in the driveway. You wish now that you had stayed home and arranged to help Andy some other day. Your wife approaches you as you enter the house.

"Where have you been? I've been miserable worrying about you. Dave called several times wanting to know where you were and said you were supposed to be home. I didn't know if you had been shot or what," your wife states, growing angrier by the minute.

You remember turning off the radio in your car when Andy was with you. You realize that Dave may have tried to contact you on the radio.

"I was with Andy, getting the gun permit I promised him," you sheepishly try to explain.

Your wife begins to explain that Dave wants you to call him. Apparently something is wrong at the surveillance site and you are needed. As you reach for the telephone to call Dave, your wife makes another comment.

"Before you call and rush out again, let me tell you something. I can't take anymore of this. I am worried about Billy and I am sick of the way your work dominates our lives. It has come to the point that you're going to have to decide between your big important investigations or us. I mean it, I'll take Billy and leave you," your wife warns, tears streaming down her face.

You find yourself feeling more frustrated than angry. Dave is waiting for your call. Your family is waiting for your time. You have got to make some hard decisions.

Based on what you have read, answer the following questions:

1. Describe your portrayal in this case in terms of being a police officer, family man, and describe your general disposition.

2. Briefly, discuss your point of view. Discuss your wife's point of view.

3. What would you do, as the officer? What resources are available to you? To your wife?

CASE 5
CIVIL LIABILITY

You have just placed an intoxicated driver under arrest. Having handcuffed the subject's hands behind his back and placed him in the cage car, you notify headquarters that you have a prisoner in custody and are en route to the city jail. The man you have just arrested is an attorney in your city. The man's name is Jefferson, and he specializes in civil law. You are aware of Jefferson's reputation as being an "ambulance chaser" who obtains clients by talking them into suing. You do not like his type of attorney, and you are rather pleased with yourself for arresting him on a DWI charge.

Jefferson is not very drunk but has had enough to drink to render him legally intoxicated. He is very upset at you and has been making threatening remarks to you.

"I'm not going to sit still for this. I'm not drunk. I only had a couple of drinks at a party. I'll have you in court for this," Jefferson continues.

You do not respond to Jefferson's threats but just glare at him in the rearview mirror and smile to yourself.

"Mr. Jefferson, you'll have to submit to an intoximeter test when I get to the jail," you advise.

"I'm not going to take an intoximeter test," Jefferson responds.

"Well, you don't have to, but you may lose your driver's license under the Implied Consent Law," you add.

"Look, don't tell me about the law. I'm an attorney, I know what the law says. I want to take a blood analysis test and not an intoximeter test," Jefferson tells you.

According to your state law, an individual arrested on a DWI charge has the right to refuse a breath analysis test and request a blood analysis test. The blood analysis is more accurate than the intoximeter test. A qualified doctor or nurse must administer the blood test, however. The hospital is several miles from your location, and it will take quite a while to arrive at the hospital. Also, the hospital emergency room is frequently busy and usually you must wait several minutes before a nurse can administer a blood test on a DWI offender.

"He's killing time so he can sober up," you think to yourself.

"OK, Mr. Jefferson. A blood test it is," you state as you turn your cruiser around and head toward the hospital.

Jefferson is still threatening you with civil action for false arrest as you explain your situation on the radio to headquarters. You have been lucky so far in your police career. You have never been sued. Some police officers have told you that a cop is not doing his job if he has not been sued. Civil action against police is popular and sometimes profitable. You know several officers who have had to pay out of their own pocket in civil actions against them.

Just as you are turning onto the street leading to the hospital, a car backs out of a driveway into your path. You slam on the brakes to avoid hitting the backing vehicle. Jefferson, unable to catch himself with his hands cuffed behind him, strikes his head against the cage frame in the back seat of your cruiser. You look into the back seat and see Jefferson trying to get back into the seat.

"You alright, Mr. Jefferson?" you ask in a concerned manner.

Jefferson does not acknowledge your question. He looks at you and begins to smile. Blood is trickling from Jefferson's nose, and there is a large bruise on his cheek.

"This'll cost you, son. You shouldn't have hit me. That's police brutality," Jefferson states with confidence.

You do not say anything and continue toward the hospital. You notice that Jefferson has stopped threatening to sue you.

"He doesn't have to threaten now, he's going to do it," you think to yourself.

As you pull into the hospital parking area, Jefferson asks you a question.

"Son, we can forget this whole thing. All you have to do is drive me back to my car and let me go home and I won't say anything about it. If you'll drop the DWI charge, I won't sue. Believe me, if I sue you I'll win. Especially with my bloody nose and bruised face. You'll be paying me for the rest of your life and all I'll get is a small fine. What do you say?"

Based on what you have read, answer the following questions:

1. Could Mr. Jefferson sue you? Do you think Mr. Jefferson would win a judgment? Even if Mr. Jefferson lost the civil case, would it hurt the police image in the public eye?

2. What would you do as the officer in this case?

3. If Mr. Jefferson sued you, what defense evidence could you produce?

CASE 6
THE SCHOOL OF HARD KNOCKS

You have recently been assigned to Delgado High School. The chief recommended you for the assignment because, according to him, you are both . . ."a woman and a damn fine officer!" After having been on patrol for eight years, you had felt you were ready for a change—but now you aren't sure you are ready for this much change.

Delgado High had gone through a very traumatic incident a year earlier. A group of three boys who were juniors and two sophomore girls had terrorized the high school by setting fire to the principal's office and attempting to assassinate an assistant principal, a history teacher, and a physical education teacher. The leader of the group, who dressed in black and referred to himself as the "Dark Side," was a senior who was not involved in the attack but believed by many to have planned it and encouraged the others to carry it out. The result was senseless violence. Mr. Simms, the history teacher, was killed by a shotgun blast while teaching a class. Two other students in his class were also wounded, one seriously. At the same time this was happening, the principal's office was set on fire by a Molotov cocktail. The principal had stepped out of his office moments before the attack, but his secretary, who was due to retire at the end of the year, was severely burned. The assailants had worn ski masks but were easily recognized by several students to whom they had bragged about the impending assault. As police arrived on the scene, one of the male students committed suicide. The others quickly surrendered and are now awaiting trial. The ringleader and his family had left the area, but he is also scheduled to go to trial at a later date on a lesser charge. Needless to say, students, parents and the community in general are still traumatized and upset about the violence. Your job, as well as that of your two fellow officers, is to reassure students and their families that the high school is a safe and secure environment.

At first, you relished the challenge and believed you could really make a difference. Now, you aren't so sure. Part of the problem involves your fellow officers. Ned is a year away from retirement and does no more than he has to. In fact, you have caught him napping in the gym on two occasions. Jack, a rookie in his first year of policing, seems more interested in flirting with the girls and impressing the guys with his police savvy than in doing a good job. Mr. Evans, the guidance counselor, has come to you and requested that you assist him in coming up with a plan to help students and families recover from the tragedy, and the chief has given his OK. Mr. Evans has asked you and your two fellow officers to provide more coverage of the school, including night classes. He also wants you to prepare several lecture/discussion sessions for students on recognizing violence-prone persons, preventing violence, and self-defense. Although you respect Mr. Evans and feel his requests are reasonable, your two partners aren't very enthusiastic; with one exception: Jack has indicated that he would be willing to give a karate demonstration to the girls' P.E. class.

You are beginning to feel caught in the middle. On one hand, it is obvious to you that many students are still nervous and anxious about the violence that happened a year ago, and according to Mr. Evans, parents are also anxious and jumpy. In fact, he has indicated that when any altercation occurs, many parents tend to keep the children home for a day or two. On the other hand, you and your fellow officers have received no special training for this type of situation, and your partners don't have the best of attitudes. You want to put together a plan that will be useful to Mr. Evans and meaningful to students and their parents, but you know that for the plan to be effective, it will have to strike the right balance.

Based on what you have read, answer the following questions:

1. Is the police chief responsible for the attitude of the two less enthusiastic officers? If so, in what ways?

2. Should students, parents, and teachers be involved in any way in developing the plan? If so, how? Give examples.

3. What might be some long-term security and safety goals for Delgado High School?

CASE 7
TO PROTECT AND SERVE

You are a rookie police officer preparing for your first tour of duty. You have just finished an intensive ten-week training session that is supposed to prepare you for every aspect of police work. You have a lot to remember and, just to be sure, you have brought along your academy notebook for reference.

It is getting close to roll-call time, and you grab your gunbelt from your locker and run toward a roll-call room. You wonder which of the officers at roll call will be your partner as you look around at their faces. You are almost late and decide to sit at the back of the room so as not to attract attention to yourself.

"Patrolman Shipley, Unit 17-Baker, your new partner is a rookie named Wallace, William C. Good luck," the sergeant announces with a laugh.

You strain to see what Officer Shipley looks like but cannot because of your seat position. The roll-call sergeant finishes his announcements and dismisses the shift. You notice that you forgot your academy notebook back in the locker room. You run back to the locker room, then out to the police parking lot.

Opening the passenger door of Unit 17-Baker, you see that Officer Shipley is already sitting on the passenger side. Shipley is a big man in his late fifties and appears friendly as he looks up at you and smiles. "Get in on the other side, kid; I don't feel like driving today," says Shipley as he closes his door.

You introduce yourself to your new partner as you start the cruiser toward your assigned beat. Shipley begins to explain the beat to you, the people, the places, and what to watch out for. Shipley has very definite opinions about police work and does not hesitate telling you what they are. He talks about how persons in the community you serve do not respect the police.

"They don't think we're human; all they see is the uniform," Shipley explains. Shipley goes on to say that the community often complains about police action. You remember the psychology and sociology topics at the police academy and the discussions about handling verbal abuse from community members.

"Everybody gets upset when they get speeding or parking tickets; they have to take it out on somebody and we're just handy," you explain to Shipley.

"It's not just speeding and parking tickets, kid; most people don't appreciate what we're trying to do."

You look at Shipley with a puzzled expression and decide to change the subject.

"When did you go to the police academy, Tom?"

"Didn't have an academy when I started. They just pinned a badge on you, gave you a gun and told you to go out and enforce the law. The streets were our training academy."

"So, how long have you been with the department?" you ask, thinking that Shipley must be ancient.

"I started in '63, the day after my 21st birthday," states Shipley proudly.

"You ought to be retired by now. That's over 33 years ago," you respond.

"Yeah, I could retire. Some of the guys I started with retired a few years ago. Poor souls. Some of 'em turned to the bottle, one committed suicide, most of 'em just waiting around to die. That's not for me. I'll work until they carry me out. Thank God there's no mandatory retirement here."

After an hour and a half of listening to Shipley talk about the old days and the complete history of the police department, you again decide to try to change the subject.

"My wife and I are going to a party next Friday night with some old friends of mine. You want to come with us?" you ask Shipley, really hoping that he will refuse.

"No thanks, kid; the only parties I go to are the F.O.P. parties. I also go out once in awhile with some old police buddies. You ought to join the F.O.P., they have some good get-togethers. I'll bring you an application if you want."

You smile at Shipley, thinking how it would be to spend your free time with the same people you had to work with. You are not sure you would like it.

"Don't you have any friends that aren't cops?" you ask Shipley.

"Sure, but not many. I don't feel as comfortable around them as I do fellow cops. Anyways, regular people don't want cops as friends, unless they want tickets fixed or something. You'll find that out soon enough."

Shipley's words really begin to bother you. It seems evident that Shipley does not care about anyone except fellow cops. You always believed that the police were supposed to protect and serve the public. Surely that does not mean that the police are supposed to avoid the public socially. You start remembering all those general orders the police department made you memorize at the academy. "Officers should not frequent bars, become intoxicated in public, and must act in a responsible and official manner at all times." In other words, you are a police officer twenty-four hours day. But these orders do not mean that you cannot have fun and be sociable with people.

It is now Friday afternoon and you are getting off duty. You have learned a lot during the past week riding with Shipley. He may be old fashioned in his ways of dealing with people, but he has a lot of experience from which you can learn. You think of how much more you have learned in the past week than during the entire ten weeks at the academy. As you head for home, you look forward to tonight's party and begin to think how nice it will be to see your old friends again.

That evening, as you and your wife pull up in front of your friend's house, you see that the party has already started. It is always good to be fashionably late, you think to yourself as you knock on the door. Your friend has a nice home and makes a good living as an automobile salesman. You have not seen him or any of your other friends since you joined the police force. The door opens and your friend and his wife greet you and ask you in. Your friend goes to the kitchen to fix you and your wife a drink as you go around saying hello to all your other friends at the party.

"Putting any crooks in jail these days?" asks your friend while handing you a drink.

You start to tell him about the drunk you arrested the other day but decide not to after seeing several of your friends at the party well on their way to intoxication.

"No, not yet. But give me time, I'm sure to catch a murderer or two," you jokingly respond.

After a couple of hours, you notice that several of your friends have already asked you to fix parking tickets, asked your opinion on legal issues, and even asked if you mind if they smoked pot at the party. Other party goers seem more distant, even uncomfortable when they learn of your profession. Tom Shipley's words again return to your consciousness . . . "Regular people don't want cops as friends . . ."

As the party continues, you become increasingly aware that things are different now that you are a police officer. Perhaps some of what Shipley said was true. The question is, how are you going to handle it? You do not intend to give up your chosen profession but are not sure how to put your nonpolice relationships in an appropriate perspective.

Based on what you have read, answer the following questions:

1. Why do you think the community isolates the police?
2. Does the community stereotype police officers?
3. Would you, as the officer, attempt to "break the barrier" between you and your friends or would you seek new police friendships? If you found no barrier between yourself and your friends at the party, do you think the friendships would last?

CASE 8
OFF DUTY OR OFF LIMITS?

"What goes around comes around. If it sounds too good to be true, it probably is. There are no free lunches." All of these thoughts float around in your head and mingle with the smoke and noise from the jukebox blaring a Bob Seger song on a hot July night at the Renegade Lounge. The bar's owner, Antonio Carimi, has just come up to you and requested that you and a couple of your friends throw out—or better yet, arrest—the two rednecks in the back booth who are heckling Lou Lou, his best waitress—but not before you give them a good ass kicking. Apparently they have been making fun of everything from Lou Lou's name to her weight. The final straw for both Antonio and his waitress was when the more inebriated of the two occupants of the booth had thrown a handful of peanuts at Lou Lou and called her a pig. At that point Antonio approached them, and the result was that they also included him in their barrage of insults, including the statement, "We'll make you an offer that you can't refuse. Go get us another pitcher of the rotgut beer you serve at this poor excuse of a bar!" Antonio had endured all he could stand.

Antonio, himself a former cop, had made his lounge like a second home for you and the officers from the third precinct. Free food, free beer, and a room in the back, complete with shower, afforded you and your friends a place to eat, relax, and socialize. In fact, last year at Thanksgiving when you were alone, you had dropped by the lounge for a quick sandwich and much to your surprise found half a dozen other police officers enjoying a traditional Thanksgiving spread, compliments of Antonio. Several hours later, after coffee and pumpkin pie, you and your compatriots had watched a bowl game on the Renegade's big screen television.

Now, Antonio expected some reciprocation.

Unfortunately, you and your drinking buddies, Tom and Jimmy, are yourselves a little intoxicated. You are also off duty and dressed in civilian clothes. After checking out the two brash fellows in the back booth, you realize they are more than a little intoxicated and would most likely put up a fight if confronted. You relay Antonio's request to your two friends. Tom doesn't want to get involved, since he is planning on going home to his wife and kids after he finishes his drink. Jimmy, on the other hand, is ready to "whup ass," compliments of about three beers too many. Antonio is eyeing you from the bar, waiting for you to take care of his problem.

Based on what you have read, answer the following questions:

1. If you were Antonio, would you expect the three officers to help you out?

2. Why would the officer in question be reluctant to intervene?

3. What might be some legal ramifications if the police officers accede to Antonio's request?

Section VI

POLICE ETHICS

Introduction

Police ethics involve a broad spectrum of behavior that includes not only corruption but also malpractice, mistreatment of offenders, racial discrimination, illegal searches and seizures, suspects' constitutional rights violations, perjury, evidence planting, and other misconduct committed under the authority of law enforcement.

Various forms of police ethics exist and are influenced by numerous factors. For instance, one might distinguish between the overzealous narcotics officer who plants evidence on suspects and the corrupt narcotics officer who takes bribes to forego enforcement of the law. Regardless of the motivations, when police officers violate their professional responsibility to uphold the law, they create image problems both within the police department and within the community. The violation of police ethics affects the public image of all police officers, eroding the public's confidence in the police profession and increasing the difficulties encountered on the job.

The police profession is unlike other vocations in a number of ways, all of which contribute to the problem of police malpractice and the number of citizen complaints regarding police actions. Some of the factors that influence police misconduct and the frequency of complaints against police officers include:

1. Because police have the unique responsibility for law enforcement, they are sometimes asked by others to ignore violations of the law for one reason or another.

2. Most police are visible in their uniforms and in their vehicles, making their actions—both good and bad—more noticeable to the public.

3. Enforcement of the law often creates resentment that sometimes becomes vindictive and personal.

4. Police officers are exposed to temptations not often found in other forms of work.

5. Officers in the field usually work without direct supervision, a fact that creates additional opportunity for misconduct and unethical practices.

6. The public tends to be more critical of police because the police are expected to exhibit a higher level of conduct and behavior than others. When they do not exhibit this higher degree of good conduct, complaints may be expected.

7. The nature of police work occasionally attracts persons who have antisocial or brutal tendencies, which creates a need for psychological screening.

8. The emotional charge of situations is frequently encountered during police contacts such as arrest, interviews at crime scenes, and so on. Such intense emotion can obscure reason and judgment of both police officers and citizens (Fyfe, Greene, and Walsh, 1999).

Degrees of Police Ethics

While the public may disagree or be unfamiliar with what constitutes police malpractice and ethics, the police cannot afford the same luxury. There are degrees of wrongdoing that must be defined and prohibited by police agencies. There are three basic forms of police malpractice: (1) legalistic, (2) professional, and (3) moralistic (Barker, 1993).

Legalistic malpractice may also be referred to as police corruption. Varying degrees and types of police corruption exist in nearly all police agencies. Police corruption includes: (1) the misuse of police authority for personal gain; (2) activity of the police that compromises their ability to enforce the law or provide police services impartially; (3) the protection of illegal activities from police enforcement; and (4) the police involvement in promoting the business of one while discouraging that of another. Police corruption is defined, therefore, as "acts" involving the misuse of authority by a police officer in a manner designed to produce personal gain for oneself or for others. Even this definition produces a problem of "where to draw the line." A police officer who frequently eats at a restaurant where he/she receives free meals or is given a discount because he/she is a police officer would constitute police corruption under this definition.

Professional malpractice can range from physical and verbal abuse of an individual to "conduct unbecoming an officer." Physical abuse may exhibit the characteristics of police brutality and use of excessive force in arresting a suspect. Verbal abuse may display characteristics of improper communication with suspects and witnesses; the violation of civil rights in interrogations with accused individuals; or sexual harassment of suspects, victims and even fellow co-workers (Rubin, 1995). Professional malpractice may take two basic forms: one of law, and one of professional conduct. Illegal conduct would include excessive physical force and violation of civil rights. Professional misconduct would include improper police behaviors (i.e., police officers drinking alcoholic beverages in the public view).

Moralistic malpractice includes the discretionary powers of police officers. Personal feelings, prejudices, and friendships may influence a police officer's decision regarding whether to take police action or to ignore situations that warrant such actions. A police officer may feel that a person or group of persons are more deserving of police attention than others. Police officers may consciously and unconsciously label and stereotype certain types of individuals as being good or bad. Such attitudes may cause a police officer to look more closely for violations by one type of individual while only giving a cursory glance at others. A police officer may decide to arrest one type of individual because they are "deserving of it," while deciding not to arrest another type of individual because they are "all right."

Social and Psychological Influences on Police Ethics

It has often been said that nothing is wrong with the police profession that is not wrong with the entire society. Law enforcement does not exist in a vacuum. The police profession represents a cross-section of the community. In communities where the majority of the population are not prejudiced, one might expect to find very little prejudice in the police. Police officers in highly prejudiced communities are rewarded for their prejudiced attitudes by the general population and therefore may often find it beneficial to exhibit such attitudes (Rhoades, 1991).

Police officers do not enjoy the prestige, salary, dignity, or esteem that they believe their profession deserves. Police officers face complex situations daily that are perplexing, frustrating, and, at times, dangerous. A police officer's education and training often does not adequately prepare him or her to face responsibilities with enough confidence. There are few police agencies that provide enlightened leadership and clear policies. Most police officers are left to make their own decisions, often without proper guidance. Police officers are seldom praised for their good deeds but are quickly reminded of their bad ones. Police officers often find it difficult to enforce laws or professionally assert themselves with upper-class citizens. This leaves only the lower and middle classes, especially minorities, with which to enforce the full authority of the law. These groups seldom have the influential lines of communication to those in power who may give them relief from police actions.

The complex nature of law enforcement and the myriad problems the police face require a tremendous number of discretionary decisions. As noted previously, few police agencies have clear policy guidelines or enlightened supervision. Without such, the police officer is under substantial stress to act or not to act in given situations. If the officer takes action, will he/she be ostracized? If the officer does not take action, will he/she be criticized for not performing his/her job properly?

Many police administrators have stated, "the public gets the kind of law enforcement they want," or "the people don't want good law enforcement." These statements reflect the social influences on police actions. The influential elements of a community, the more socially and economically powerful citizens, are often in a position to direct and dictate police actions. These are the groups that typically comprise the leaders and respected citizens of a community. It is not uncommon for these groups to advocate quality law enforcement as long as the enforcement does not interfere with their lives.

Political Influence on Police Ethics

Most recruits enter the police profession with an idealistic attitude. Most of them believe police work involves keeping the peace, protecting citizens from criminal activity, and preserving the social order. While such an idealistic attitude has some merit, many officers change their attitude regarding police work after a relatively short time on the job. Many officers find that an unwritten policy of discrimination exists concerning police work. Officers become frustrated when tickets are fixed or prominent citizens are treated too generously by the courts. Officers also become frustrated when they find injustice within the criminal justice system. Officers often become demoralized when they invest their time and risk their lives to make an arrest and find that the offender is given a minimum sentence. Such frustration can easily lead a police officer to assume a more realistic attitude regarding police work. The officer finds that police work is a part of our democratic society that tends to tolerate a variety of injustices (Girodo, 1991). As a result, some police officers may resort to unethical police procedures, corruption, and even close their eyes to violations of the law (Barker, 1993). Such police actions may result in an increase in using "drop guns," excessive force, violating constitutional rights of offenders, planting evidence, acceptance of bribes, and discriminatory enforcement of the law (Barker and Carter, 1990; Roberg, Crank, and Kuykendall, 2000).

Improving Police Ethics

There is a need for change in the police profession. Not all police officers are unethical, and not all police officers who are unethical necessarily prefer it that way (Miller and Braswell, 1985). Social and political influences on the police profession may create a polarization regarding police ethics. When such influences dictate police actions, some actions may become ethical because they conform to the reality of the system. Those within the system that oppose the influences become outsiders and are thus viewed as unethical (Maas, 1973). Therefore, it may become unprofessional or unethical to, relatively speaking, initiate police action or arrest a member of the upper class, a politician, a judge, or even a fellow police officer.

Police ethics can be improved in a number of ways, including the following:

1. Improved selection and screening techniques for persons entering police service and, especially, those selected for leadership positions.

2. Increasingly stringent personnel requirements, such as advanced education and formal training including the encouragement of higher education for in-service police ethics.

3. Basic research and development in police organizations, policy-setting techniques, and community attitudes toward the police.

4. Policy guideline formulation and training in policy application and practice within the department.

5. More control over discretionary decision making by police officers.

6. Facilitating change of citizen perspective of the police by developing supportive services within the community as well as the department.

7. Increased review of police actions by independent agencies and media representatives knowledgeable of the police profession (Scrivner, 1994; Kleinig, 1997; Braswell, McCarthy, and McCarthy, 1998).

Summary

Police ethics include a broad range of police behavior and "misbehavior," including corruption, discrimination, violation of constitutional and civil rights, and other police misconduct. Various forms of police malpractice include mitigating as well as aggravating circumstances. For instance, many police officers may condemn fellow officers for being corrupt, while dismissing practices of perjury, gratuity acceptance, and evidence planting as a necessary part of the police job or as a fringe benefit of policing. In the final analysis, there seem to be degrees of police ethics in malpractice ranging from major offenses to minor infractions or even acceptable behavior. There are both social and political influences on police ethics that may increase or decrease police malpractice. When the community is corrupt, the police department often follows the same inclination. If political pressures influence the population and other organizations within the community, one may be assured that the same political pressures will influence police actions or nonactions. Unethical police practices can be decreased by increased monitoring of police actions by the public as well as more stringent selection and promotion procedures of police personnel.

References

Barker, T., and D. Carter (1993). "Fluffing up the Evidence and Covering Your Ass: Some Conceptual Notes on Police Lying." *Deviant Behavior*, 11(1): 61–73.

———. (1986). *Police Deviance*. Cincinnati: Anderson Publishing Co.

Braswell, M. McCarthy, B. and McCarthy, B. (1998). *Justice Crime and Ethics*, 3d ed. Cincinnati: Anderson Publishing Co.

Fyfe, J., J. Greene, and W. Walsh. (1997). *Police Administration*, 5th ed. New York: McGraw-Hill.

Girodo, M. (1991). "Drug Corruption in Undercover Agents: Measuring the Risk," *Behavioral Sciences and the Law*, 9(3): 361–370.

Kleinig, J. (1997). "Teaching and Learning Police Ethics: Competing and Complimentary Approaches." *Journal of Criminal Justice*, 18(1): 1–18.

Maas, P. (1973). *Serpico*. New York: The Viking Press.

Miller, L., and M. Braswell (1985). "Teaching Police Ethics: An Experiential Model," *American Journal of Criminal Justice*, 10 (Fall).

Rhoades, P. (1991). "Political Obligation: Connecting Police Ethics and Democratic Values." *American Journal of Police,* 10(2): 1–22.

Roberg, R., J. Crank, and J. Kuykendall. (2000). *Police and Society*, 2d ed. Los Angeles: Roxbury Publishing Co.

Rubin, P. (1995). "Civil Rights and Criminal Justice: Primer on Sexual Harassment." *Research in Action*, October. Washington, DC: National Institute of Justice.

Scrivner, E. (1994). "Controlling Police Use of Excessive Force: The Role of the Police Psychologist." *Research in Action*, October. Washington, DC: National Institute of Justice.

CASES INVOLVING POLICE ETHICS

Members of the police profession have, perhaps, more power than any other component of the criminal justice system. Police officers possess the discretion to make an arrest or to ignore criminal activity. This power attracts many police applicants. It also attracts attention from professional criminals, politicians, business people, and the "man next door" who wants a ticket fixed.

It is not only corruption that destroys the police image. Unethical procedures utilized to bring a law breaker to justice also have a devastating effect upon the public's view of law enforcement.

In the following eight cases, you will have the opportunity to make decisions regarding corruption and ethics. You must be able to define police corruption in your own terms and decide what is ethical or unethical in each situation presented.

Case number one, "Fringe Benefits," involves a rookie police officer who is realizing that law enforcement work may bring many unexpected benefits. "Police discounts" may be one method the public uses to thank police officers for performing their duty. These discounts also may be the means to provide police officers with the incentives not to perform their duty.

Case number two, "Corrupt Community—Corrupt Police," explores the relationship between the elected law enforcement administrator and the constituency. A newly elected sheriff is faced with an important decision. Should he enforce the law in his county or bow to the political pressures of certain community members? If he enforces the law, he may not be re-elected. If he performs selectively, the way the citizens want, he will perpetuate a tradition of corruption.

Case number three, "Super Cop," deals with the methods of solving crimes some police officers utilize. One of the best police officers on the force is using unethical techniques to solve crimes. By using these techniques, the officer is solving crimes and getting sound convictions. When another officer questions his methods, the other department members advise him that "that's the way it is."

Case number four, "Drop Gun," involves a police officer who has questioned his partner about the use of a "drop gun" in a shooting incident. The partner advises him that if he doesn't use the drop gun, it could mean a civil suit and even his job. The officer is now faced with a choice between going to his superiors about his partner's use of the drop gun or remaining silent.

Case number five, "Employment or Ethics?" deals with a police officer who has stopped the mayor's son for drunken driving. Weighing all the consequences, the officer decides it is his duty to make an arrest. Later, the chief of police advises the officer to drop the charges or face the possibility of termination.

Case number six, "Constitutional Rights," discusses how the police "get around" the legal requirements of rights of the accused. A newly appointed police detective finds that not every suspect receives their right to remain silent or to have an attorney present during questioning. A veteran police detective shows the young officer how to "get around" the constitutional rights requirement with suspects.

Case number seven, "Sexual Harassment," concerns a rookie police officer being sexually harassed by a commanding officer. The rookie officer must decide whether to bring the commander up on charges or handle the situation in a more informal manner. The problem is especially troublesome since the rookie is an African-American male and the commander is a white female.

Case number eight, "The Transmission of Justice," puts a police officer on the spot. He helped a businessman's son gain pretrial diversion, as he would have any juvenile in a similar circumstance. In appreciation, the father wouldn't accept payment for the repair on the officer's vehicle. Now, the son is in trouble again and his father wants the officer's help.

CASE 1
FRINGE BENEFITS

Crawling into the passenger side of a patrol car, you position yourself beside your new partner, Bert Thompson. You have been working in the city jail as a detention officer since you graduated from the police academy three weeks ago. It is standard policy for your department to have new officers work inside prior to patrol duty.

"Name's Bert. Bet you're glad to get out of jail duty and onto some patrol," Bert remarks with a big grin.

"Sure am. My name's Warren," you reply.

"OK, Warren, let's go fight crime," says Bert as he pulls out of the parking lot.

Bert breaks the silence. "Warren, it's almost eight-thirty and looks like our side of town is pretty slow this morning. How about a cup of coffee?"

"Fine, there's a coffee shop over there," you point out.

"No, no, not that place. Higher than a cat's back on prices. I know this doughnut place just up the road," Bert says.

Bert pulls into a franchised coffee and doughnut shop and tells you to wait in the cruiser and monitor the calls from headquarters.

"How do you like your coffee, Warren?" Bert asks as he steps out of the car.

"Black," you respond.

You see Bert through the large windows of the doughnut shop joking with one of the waitresses as he orders the coffee. You notice the waitress handing a large bag to Bert and begin to wonder how much coffee he bought. "What did you do, buy out the whole place?" you ask as Bert climbs back into the cruiser.

"Well, I thought a few doughnuts wouldn't hurt along with our coffee," Bert says as he takes coffee cups from the bag.

"How much I owe you for mine?" you ask Bert.

"Not a thing. This was on the house, if you know what I mean," Bert responds with a grin.

"They told us at the academy we weren't supposed to take gratuities or anything like that," you state, trying to remain objective.

"Look Warren, on the salaries we make and the type of work we do, it's not a gratuity to take an occasional free ride. Most merchants in the community enjoy giving the cops a free meal or a discount now and then—it makes them feel like they can contribute. When we eat lunch today we'll get it for free or at least at a discount. Restaurant owners like to see cops in their establishments. It makes for good business."

"Yeah, but what if they want something in return?" you ask.

"Warren, in twelve years of police work I've had maybe two or three ask me for a favor. Anyway, they weren't big things—fixing tickets, and stuff like that," Bert responds patiently.

Bert's argument seems pretty convincing. After all, Bert says that everyone in the department does it to some extent, including the chief.

That night, as you prepare to go to your night class at the university, you check your work schedule for the next month and notice that you will be rotating to the 3–11 shift in three weeks.

Rotating onto the afternoon-evening shift poses a problem for you. You are working on an associate's degree at the university and are going to two night classes a week. Rotating to the 3–11 shift means that you will miss two weeks of classes. It is too late in the semester to drop the classes without penalty, so you decide to talk with the instructors concerning your problem.

Your first instructor, Dr. Whitaker, was very understanding and provided you with a research paper assignment to make up for the lost time. You have one more instructor to contact.

"Dr. Rowland, I'm sorry but I've been switched over to an evening shift and I'll have to miss the next couple of classes. Is there anything I can do to make up the work that I'll miss?"

"Warren, your grades have been very good, but you know how I feel about student absenteeism. Unless you can work something out with your supervisor so that you can come to class, I would suggest that you withdraw from the course or face a serious grade reduction," Dr. Rowland suggests.

You do not want to withdraw because you currently have an A in the course and the semester will be over in six more weeks. You decide that you will talk with your lieutenant and see if you can get your off-days changed.

"No way, Warren. You know the policy. Unless there's illness or an emergency, we can't change the schedule. It would screw up the whole shift," the lieutenant explains.

A couple of days later you receive a phone call from Dr. Rowland.

"Warren, this is Jim Rowland. Did I wake you up?"

"No, Dr. Rowland, today is my day off. By the way, I guess I'll try to stick with the class and take my chances. I wasn't able to get my work schedule altered, but I figure I can take a C if I make all As and miss a couple of classes," you explain.

"Warren, I'm not calling about that but, well, I need a favor. My son got his third speeding ticket in a year yesterday, and I was wondering if there was anything you could do to help."

"Well, I don't know, Dr. Rowland. Who gave your son the ticket?" you ask reluctantly.

"An Officer Thompson. Listen, if you can help, I would certainly appreciate it. I believe I could work out your class problem and give you a final grade for the work you have already accomplished. I believe you have an A in the course up to now," Dr. Rowland adds.

Officer Thompson is Bert. It would be very easy to persuade Bert to fix the ticket and alleviate your problem with the class. By fixing the ticket you would be guaranteed an A for the course. On the other hand, you consider yourself a straight cop and not one to take payoffs. You wonder if it would be corrupt to fix the ticket. It does not really seem like such a big deal. Still, there was no mistaking what the instructor at the academy said.

Based on what you have read, answer the following questions:

1. What should you do?
2. If you refused to fix the ticket, what course grade would you likely receive? Could you seek help from other sources?
3. Discuss where an officer should "draw the line" on accepting gratuities. Is an officer corrupt when he or she accepts a free cup of coffee? Give your definition of police corruption.

CASE 2
CORRUPT COMMUNITY—
CORRUPT POLICE

As newly elected sheriff of a small rural county, you were extensively supported by the news media and influential people of the county during the campaign. Sheriff Bill Simon has a certain ring to it. Your qualifications are excellent, considering the types of sheriffs the county has had before you. You have a Bachelor's degree in Criminal Justice and seven years experience as the chief investigator for the sheriff's department. During your seven years as chief investigator, you came into contact with many people and are very much aware of the workings of your county.

During your campaign for sheriff, you promised to uphold the law and to enforce it to the best of your ability if elected. You promised to run the sheriff's department in an ethical and professional manner and to keep the office free from corruption. Now that you have been elected, you intend to stand by those campaign promises and develop your department into a professional law enforcement organization.

Shortly after becoming sheriff, many of your campaign supporters came to you requesting jobs as deputies or for deputy sheriff identification cards. You expected this and were not too concerned. After all, you should employ qualified individuals as deputies and give reserve deputy sheriff cards to those you trust.

Several upstanding members of church organizations visited you and called for action on vice and immoral businesses operating in your county. You began to respond to the fullest legal extent of the law against massage parlors and adult book stores in the county. These businesses are considered "shady operations" and are the source of many law enforcement problems in the county. One adult book store could not take the "heat" you were putting on them and had to fold. You arrested the owner of one of the massage parlors for attempted bribery when he offered you five thousand dollars to "look the other way" regarding some of his illegal activities.

The news media and the community are supportive of your position against the massage parlors and adult book stores. You feel that you are beginning to live up to your campaign promises.

One day, one of your deputies informs you of certain illegal gambling operations in the county. Apparently some of the fraternal clubs in the county are operating slot machines and holding high-stakes poker games. Your deputy has enough information to obtain a search warrant on one of the clubs—a veterans' organization. After reviewing his evidence you decide to make a raid on the club.

Your raid is very successful. Twenty-two slot machines and several thousand dollars of poker money is confiscated. Eighteen persons are arrested for illegal gambling operations.

The next morning you receive a visitor in your office. The visitor is Max Snelling, one of your stronger campaign supporters and a retired criminal court justice.

"Morning, Sheriff Simon. I'd like to talk with you for a moment if you're not too busy," Max asks with a smile.

"Hey, I've always got time for you, Judge, after all the support you gave me during my campaign," you respond, shaking Max's hand.

"Sheriff, it's about that raid last night on the Vets Club. Now you know I don't like to get politically involved in such things, but I got a lot of phone calls last night. You know, it's hard being a retired judge when people continue to contact you about their problems. It seems a lot of folks want to know whether or not you are going to continue raiding fraternal clubs."

"Not if I don't have to, Judge. If these clubs don't learn to obey the state law against gambling, then they're just as illegal as massage parlors and dope pushers," you respond.

"I know, Sheriff, but this is a little different. You've got a lot of people worried that you're going to raid some of the other fraternal clubs in the county. Some of those people are pretty influential and helped to get you elected. John Phelps, publisher of the newspaper, belongs to one club, and countless county officials are members of almost all the fraternal clubs here."

"There's nothing different about the law, Judge. You should know that. If those places are involved in illegal activities, then I will have to do something about it. I promised to uphold the law and that's what I'm going to try to do," you exclaim.

"Look, Sheriff, it's alright to bust these little shady places like massage parlors and such, because they're out in the public eye and make communities look bad, but the fraternal clubs are different. They're not open to the general public but to members only. Besides, all of them donate generously to charities and most of that money comes from the slot machines," Max explains.

"Judge, I appreciate your situation, but I promised the people of this county when I ran for sheriff that I would enforce the law, and that's what I'm doing," you argue.

"The people don't want that kind of law enforcement. They want a county sheriff who will support them, and nothing the big shots at the state capital say is going to change that. You've got to enforce the law the majority of the people want you to enforce, or you're out of office next term. It's as simple as that," Max argues.

You realize that what Max has said is probably true. If you enforce the law the way the majority of the people want you to enforce it, you could be sheriff for a long time. If you ignore what the people say and enforce the law equally, you may not be reelected.

"What it boils down to then, Judge, is I can either keep my job as sheriff or my values, but not both. Is that right?" you ask.

"I'm sorry son, that pretty much is the picture," Max states with a sad look on his face.

"What do you want me to tell the concerned citizens that are contacting me?" Max questions.

Based on what you have read, answer the following questions:

1. What should you tell Max? What should you do?
2. Would there be any difference in the situation if you were a chief of police (not an elected law enforcement official)?
3. Do you have any options that would allow you to continue to be a noncorruptible law enforcement official? List and explain.

CASE 3
SUPER COP

Bill Hammonds' name appears once again on the "Best Detective of the Month" roster. It is the sixth time in a row that Hammonds has received the honor. Hammonds was promoted from patrol to investigations just nine months ago.

"How does he do it?" you ask yourself aloud.

"Hammonds is doing a damn good job, isn't he?" Pete Rowe comments as he steps up to the bulletin board.

"That's not the word for it. Look at the difference in all of our case loads and conviction rates and then look at Hammonds'. His conviction rate is almost 80 percent while the average is around 20 percent," you point out.

"Well, I've heard that he's got a whole army of snitches working for him," Pete says as he walks away from the bulletin board.

"Snitches" is a slang word for informants. Without good informants, an investigator can do very little with an investigation. But it takes time for an investigator to develop good informants. Hammonds did not seem to have any trouble developing informants during his first weeks as an investigator. It took you almost two months to develop a couple of snitches, and Hammonds seemed to have an "army" of snitches working for him during the first several weeks of his detective assignment.

"How does he do it?" you ask yourself again.

That afternoon your captain calls you into his office.

"Mike, how's that investigation coming on the country club burglary?" the captain asks.

"It's a pretty tight case, Captain. I've got a couple of leads and I'm waiting for a response from the crime lab," you explain.

"I've been getting some pressure up the ranks to get this thing resolved. You've been working on the case for about two weeks. I'm going to put both you and Hammonds on the case and see if we can't get this thing solved," the captain says.

Walking out of the captain's office, you feel as though you have been slapped in the face. It seems obvious that the captain feels you are not as competent as Hammonds would be in solving this case. It is an insult, but one you will have to live with.

The next day, Hammonds walks up to you, sporting a grin.

"Mike, I hear you're having trouble with a burglary at the country club?" Bill asks, somewhat snidely.

"Very funny, Hammonds. C'mon, let's contact some of your snitches and see if they know anything," you retort as you grab your overcoat.

Hammonds will not allow you to talk with any of his informants. Hammonds always insists that you stay in the car while he gets out to talk. You are not very concerned because several detectives are "protective" of their sources and do not like others around while talking with them. After a while, you begin to wonder what kind of informants Hammonds has working for him. Almost all of Hammonds' snitches seem to be either drug users or pushers.

"Now all we have to do is sit back and wait for a phone call," Hammonds says as he begins to drive back to the station.

"Did any of your snitches know anything?" you ask.

"No, not yet. But one will turn up something real soon," Hammonds responds confidently.

That afternoon, Hammonds comes into the detective office with a warrant in his hand.

"This is it, Mike. I've got a warrant for Jake Lennan, the one that broke into the country club." Hammonds says as he waves the warrant in your face.

"OK, Hammonds, now tell me how you did it," you say, looking over the warrant.

"It was easy, Mike. My snitches came through with the information. Besides, I think there is a real good chance that Mr. Jake Lennan will want to talk and confess to the break-in as well as return the stolen property," Hammonds comments.

You look at Hammonds in disbelief. Hammonds, noticing the expression on your face, continues to explain.

"Look, if this Jake guy doesn't talk and confess I'd sure hate to be in his shoes when my snitches get hold of him."

Hammonds' last statement puts a thought in your mind. Apparently Hammonds is using his informants to do the investigation work for him. Hammonds' informants may even be using force on suspects like Jake Lennan to confess and return stolen property. It seems Pete was right about Hammonds having an army of snitches. You begin to wonder what Hammonds is giving his informants in return for their services.

"What're you paying your snitches for doing your work for you?" you ask with increasing skepticism.

"Nothing much. I may let them slide on a few things they may be involved with," Hammonds responds as he turns and walks away.

It is becoming more apparent to you that Hammonds may be solving cases by using his informants to do the investigation work, as well as engaging in other inappropriate activities. Hammonds' use of drug addicts and pushers as informants leads you to other possible conclusions. He could be ignoring violations of narcotics laws by his informants in return for information and services. You decide to confront Hammonds with your suspicions.

"Well, why not? I'm solving more cases than anyone else here. Why not let snitches slide on some things in return for good convictions? I haven't put one thug in jail that didn't deserve to go. It's throwing back the little fish for the big ones," Hammonds argues.

Hammonds continues to explain to you how he has been using his informants to "catch" the crooks and make them confess to their crimes.

As you think about what Hammonds said, you wonder if that is the way an investigation should be handled. His argument seems to have some merit and does produce results. It does not seem right to you that a police officer should ignore illegal activities of one group and arrest others. You decide to ask your captain.

"Look, Mike, in our business it's give and take. We have to look at our priorities. We have to look at the worst offenses and let the others slide. We can use that to our advantage the way Hammonds is doing. We've all done it as investigators—maybe not to the extent that Hammonds has, but if all of us would take that advantage, we would solve more cases," your captain explains.

The captain's statement still does not satisfy you. You still believe Hammonds' methods are unethical, even if "that's the way it is" in detective work.

You wonder what you will have to do to become "Detective of the Month."

Based on what you have read, answer the following questions:

1. Discuss the arguments of both sides for using such investigative techniques. What would you do in this situation?

2. How could a criminal investigator develop informants without using money or "promises"?

3. In your opinion, when does a police officer have justification in "throwing back the little fish" in favor of apprehending serious offenders? Explain your answer.

CASE 4
DROP GUN

You and your partner are responding to a robbery in progress call at an all-night service station. As you pull into the service station you see two black males run out the side door. Your partner jumps out of the cruiser and tells you to go around to the left side of the building as he begins to run toward the right. The two subjects have split up and you are now pursuing the one who ran toward the left. Spotting the subject trying to hide in some brush, you pull your pistol and shine your flashlight on the subject.

"OK, come on out. Don't make me have to start shooting," you warn.

The youth steps out of the bushes with his hands raised. You handcuff the subject and search him. You find a toy pistol in the subject's back pocket.

"This what you used to try and rob the place?" you ask, holding the toy pistol in the youth's face.

"All we had, man. Can't afford no real gun," the youth responds.

You lead the subject over to the cruiser and place him in the back seat. You walk into the service station and see a middle-aged man wiping perspiration from his forehead with a handkerchief. You ask the man if he is uninjured.

"Yeah, I'm OK, Officer. I see you got one of them," he replies.

Suddenly, you hear three gunshots ring out and become concerned about your partner. Running out of the service station toward the area where the shots came from, you hear a fourth gunshot. After running a couple of hundred feet, you see your partner standing over the body of the second youth.

"What happened, Jim?" you ask your partner.

"Damned kid pulled a gun on me, had to shoot him," your partner replies, his eyes wide with fear.

You kneel down beside the body and confirm the youth is dead. You pick up the small handgun laying next to the body. The handgun is a cheap blue steel .25 caliber automatic with white plastic grips. The weapon had apparently been fired once, as you notice one shell-casing on the ground.

"Couldn't help it. I cornered the kid here and he swung around at me with that gun. I shot three times and he shot once into the ground. I guess I'm pretty lucky," your partner explains.

"You sure are. You know, this gun looks like that one you took off of that guy in the park last month," you comment.

"Well, you know about those types of guns. They're floating around everywhere," your partner responds.

You remember what the other youth said about not having enough money to buy a real gun and the fact that he had a toy pistol on him.

"Jim, I caught the other kid and he had a toy gun on him. He said that they didn't have a real gun," you state, looking to see what your partner's reaction will be.

"Hey, look, you're my partner. We've got to stick together on this. I'll level with you. This kid didn't have a gun; it was dark and he jumped out of the bushes here trying to run away. It startled me and I shot him. After I noticed he didn't have a gun I put that .25 in the kid's hand and shot into the ground. I've been carrying that .25 just in case something like this happened," your partner explains.

"Jim, you don't have to use a drop gun. It was just an accident. I'd have shot too. You'll get in worse trouble if the boss finds out you used a drop gun," you try to explain.

"No way, I'm not going to be criminally or civilly liable for shooting this thug. I could be sued, criminally charged with manslaughter, lose my job, or all three. I'm not taking any chances. I'm a cop who's just shot a kid. What do you think the media are going to do with that?" your partner explains.

What your partner did is wrong. He is right about possibly being civilly and criminally liable for his misjudgment. The same thing could have happened to you. You know that it is wrong for your partner to use a drop gun. If you go to your superiors and report the drop gun, Jim will certainly be dismissed from the department and may be criminally charged. If you say nothing and the truth comes out at a later date, you could be considered an accomplice.

Based on what you have read, answer the following questions:

1. What are you going to do?

2. If your partner did not use the "drop gun," what would be the consequences from (a) a shooting review board; (b) the news media; and (c) the community?

3. If nothing was said about the "drop gun," what would happen? Include in your discussion the internal affairs investigation steps and the probable results.

CASE 5
EMPLOYMENT OR ETHICS?

With the third blast of your siren, the black Lincoln finally pulls over against the curb. The driver is apparently intoxicated—a common occurrence on Saturday nights such as this one. You step out of your cruiser after calling in your location and the license plate of the Lincoln. Approaching the massive black car, you can see the driver is alone.

"Step out of the car, please," you politely ask the driver.

The door swings open and a young man in his late teens staggers out. The smell of beer permeates the air and an empty beer can falls from inside the Lincoln onto the pavement.

"Been drinking, son?" you ask the young driver.

"Look, don't bug me, mister. I may have had a couple, but I can handle it," the young man sullenly retorts.

Looking over the young man's driver's license, you recognize the name as being that of the son of your city's mayor.

"John P. Stone, Jr., nineteen years of age, 1633 Wessex Drive. Your father the mayor?" you ask.

"That's right, and if you know what's good for you, you'd better let me go. My dad won't appreciate one of his cops harassing me," the young man warns, becoming more belligerent.

"I'm not one of his cops. I work for the same boss he does. Besides, you can barely walk, let alone drive in your condition," you tell young Stone.

You think about driving the young man home and explaining the circumstances to Mayor Stone, but the young man's arrogance is upsetting you.

"Why should I give him a break when I would otherwise make an arrest? So what if he's the mayor's son?" you say to yourself. You could see the look of disbelief from the other officers when you took John P. Stone, Jr. down to headquarters and booked him for DWI.

Monday morning the chief of police calls you to come see him at headquarters.

"Bill, sorry to have to drag you from home early like this, but I have a problem. You arrested Mayor Stone's son Saturday night for DWI and the mayor isn't too happy about it. He wants me to try to talk you into drop-ping the charges," the chief advises you.

"Why should I, Chief? The kid was too drunk to walk. He could've killed somebody driving in that condition. I wouldn't have given anyone a break in that condition," you argue.

"Look, Bill, I'm not asking you to drop the charges, I'm telling you to. We need the mayor's support. Let me put it to you this way; you can either drop the charges or face the possibility of being fired over some-thing. I know you're a good cop, but this is a difficult situation. Believe me, if you don't drop the charges, you had best be looking for another job. The mayor has a long memory," the chief warns.

After being dismissed with the instructions to think it over, you stare at your lukewarm cup of coffee, feeling both angry and helpless. You wonder if police work is really for you.

Based on what you have read, answer the following questions:

1. What do you think the population of this city is? Would this case be different in a metropolitan-sized department? How?

2. Apparently, it is up to you to decide what to do about dropping the charges. If you refuse to drop the charges, what will most likely occur in court? What would happen to you?

3. What options do you have?

CASE 6
CONSTITUTIONAL RIGHTS

You have been transferred to the detective division in a medium-sized police department. You were a traffic patrolman for three years prior to your transfer. The only experience you have had in investigations is what you have gained in training and in accident investigations. You are excited about your transfer and are anxious to get started in criminal investigations.

Your partner is Will Madden, a veteran police detective who has been assigned to "break you in" on criminal investigation procedures. Will is somewhat gruff, in his late fifties, and has been an investigator for twenty-nine years. You feel that you are lucky to have someone like Will to give you some pointers on detective work. Will, wearing a hat that went out of style years ago, comes up to you and introduces himself.

"How ya doing, kid? Looks like it's me and you for the next few weeks," he states.

Will explains to you that he is working on an armed robbery case and has a good suspect.

"C'mon, kid. Let's go out and pick this guy up and see what he's got to say about it," Will tells you as he lights up the stub of a cigar he has been chewing on.

Driving to the suspect's residence, Will tells you some "war stories" of investigations he was involved in back during the old days.

"It must have been more exciting work back then than it is now," you comment.

"I dunno if it was more exciting or not. I know police work was easier back then. Didn't have to worry about all the paperwork and legal 'mumbo jumbo' we do now," Will remarks, chewing on his cigar.

"Here we are. Let's go see if the boy knows anything," Will states as he pulls up to the apartment building where the suspect lives.

Will knocks on the door and there is no answer. He then checks to see if the door is locked and finds that it is not.

"Let's go in and see if the boy's in bed or something," Will tells you as he enters the apartment.

"Isn't this breaking and entering illegally? I mean, we don't have a warrant or anything," you question as you follow Will inside.

"Don't worry about it, kid. Hey, I think the boy's taking a shower. I hear the water running in the bathroom," Will states as he saunters toward the sound of running water.

The suspect is taking a shower and there is no one else in the apartment. As you wait for the suspect to come out of the shower, Will searches around the apartment looking for evidence of the robbery.

"Well, look what I found. Looks like the gun the store owner described as being the one the robber used," Will says as he holds up a blue steel .45 automatic he found in a dresser drawer.

The bathroom door opens and a startled man looks at you and Will. Will is toying with the .45 automatic he found in the dresser drawer.

"How ya doing, son? Looks like your luck has run out," Will comments to the dripping man.

"What you guys doing in here? You got a warrant?" the suspect asks angrily.

"Don't need no warrant, son. I got what we call probable cause. See, you probably caused that armed robbery two nights ago and I'm holding the evidence. Now what you got to do is give back the money you stole," Will continues.

"Hey, man. You can't do this. I got rights, you know," the suspect argues.

"You ain't got no rights, boy. You can either go down hard for this or make it easy on yourself," Will advises.

The man sits down and looks very scared.

"Look, son, we got eyeball witnesses that saw you do it; we got your fingerprints; we got this gun, and now we got you. We got you good on this and it ain't no sweat off our backs if you want to cooperate or not. If you cooperate, it might relieve us of some paperwork and we'd be grateful for that. In fact, I could talk to the judge and tell him how cooperative you were and he'd probably make it easier on you. Or, I could tell him that you were uncooperative and he'd probably send you away for a long time."

The man looks worried and confused.

"Hey man, this ain't right . . ." he begins.

"It's not right or wrong, friend. That's the way it is. Now you want to cooperate or not?" Will asks.

"Sure, man. I mean, I got no choice, do I?" the man says with disgust. "Money's in the closet over there in a paper bag. Didn't even get a chance to spend any of it," the suspect comments, dejectedly looking out of a window.

Will tells you to call a cage car to transport the offender to headquarters while he searches through the closet. Finding the money, he begins to count it.

"It's all there, man. Like I said, I never had a chance to spend none of it," the man advises Will.

After the patrol car leaves the apartment building with the offender, you decide to question Will about his methods.

"Will, everything we did was in violation of that man's constitutional rights. We broke and entered his residence, made an illegal search, and questioned him without advising him of his rights. Is this how you conduct all your investigations?"

Will looked at you as an adult might look at a child.

"Look, kid, you've got a lot to learn about interrogation. We were lucky to find that gun he used in the robbery. We've got him dead to rights with that piece of evidence. Hell, I lied to him about us having eyeball witnesses and fingerprints. If he hadn't copped out, he may have gotten off with it. He'll sign a waiver of rights form when we get to headquarters and we'll get a statement from him. Besides, if he had wanted to be uncooperative and not talk, he knows we could make it rough on him. All you have to remember is when we get into court you'll say the same thing I do—that he let us in and that the gun was out in the open, we gave him his rights, and he decided to talk without a lawyer. C'mon, I'll treat you to a cup of coffee. We deserve a break."

As you leave the apartment building you consider your options—go along with Will or report him to his supervisor. You strain to think it over.

Based on what you have read, answer the following questions:

1. What constitutional rights were violated? How were they violated?

2. What would have been the proper investigative steps to take?

3. If the suspect had refused to answer questions and demanded that he be appointed a lawyer, what "pressures" could Will place on the suspect?

CASE 7
SEXUAL HARASSMENT

You are a 23-year-old African-American male who has recently graduated from the police academy. As far back as you can remember, you have always wanted to be a law enforcement officer. Despite the voices of disapproval from many of your friends and relatives, a career in law enforcement was what interested you most. Having seen how the police and the criminals operated in your neighborhood while you were growing up, you felt you could make a difference. Now is your chance. You were recently hired by the Caden Police Department, a midsized department with excellent benefits and a career ladder system.

The Caden Police Department has always had a reputation as a progressive agency. Employee benefits and salaries are much higher than those of surrounding police departments. The department even pays tuition for officers wishing to attend college, a benefit that was most attractive to you.

You were hired under a one-year probationary period like all new officers at Caden. During the probation period, you will be evaluated by numerous ranking officers to determine your suitability to become a police officer. You will finish your probationary status in six months. To date, your evaluations have been excellent and you foresee no serious problems in achieving full police officer status.

Your work during the past several weeks has been, for the most part, enjoyable. Your training officer, a middle-aged white male with some racial prejudices, seems to have finally accepted you. You can tell he still doesn't fully trust you by both what he says and doesn't say.

"You people got it made these days," he tells you. "Being black and all, I mean. The department needs to hire minorities and you probably beat out a lot of more qualified white guys," he continues. "But, all in all, you ain't so bad."

You respond by shaking your head to acknowledge that you understand what he is saying. You don't want to enter into any discussion about affirmative action, racism, reverse discrimination, or any other topic that might make your training officer angry. But the small knot in your stomach indicates something else.

In many ways, you do have it made now. A good salary and benefits have allowed your wife to quit work at the grocery store and take care of your fourteen-month-old daughter at home. You were able to buy a modest house rather than rent the one-bedroom apartment you had before being hired at the police department. You are finally working in the field you have always dreamed of.

"Yeah, I got it made now . . . almost," you say silently to yourself.

A couple of days later you get a notice to meet with Captain Irene Jamison, head of personnel and training in your department. Captain Jamison is a slightly overweight white female in her mid-thirties. She is married to a much older man who happens to be a city commissioner and is active in local and state politics. Word among the other officers is that she got her job and rank because of her husband.

"She'll probably be chief before long," your training officer comments to you with a sneer as you leave for your appointment.

"You wanted to see me, Captain?" you ask, after entering her office.

"Yes, Bill, I've been looking over your performance ratings and training ratings for the past six months to see if any problems have surfaced that we can catch before the end of your probationary period. I don't see anything serious, but I think we need to address a few items."

"Certainly, Captain," you state somewhat nervously.

"Bill . . . you're a good guy . . . well mannered . . . you seem to have a future here," she states, after rising to close her office door behind you.

"You know, Bill, if you play your cards right you could go places in this department . . . rank, salary, good position, maybe detective," she states, placing her hands on your shoulders while standing behind your chair.

"Well, I will certainly do my best," you stammer.

"You know, my husband is a fine and very important person. He can pull a lot of strings to get things done—at least at work if not at home, if you know what I mean," she adds with a chuckle. "I will be candid with you, Bill. I am very impressed with you . . . in every way. I think we can work something out here that will satisfy both our needs. We should get together tomorrow at my place and discuss your future in more detail and without interruptions. I'll make a change in your duty assignment so there will be no problem. Just report to me in the morning and we'll go from there. And, by the way, call me Irene," she states, returning to her chair.

"Yes sir, I mean . . . yes ma'am, Captain Irene . . . I mean . . . ." you stammer as you leave her office.

"Man, what have I gotten myself into?" you think to yourself, as you walk down the administrative office corridor. "Who does she think she is? I've got a beautiful wife and baby, I'm on probation here . . . how am I going to handle this?" you think to yourself.

What are you going to do? Telling your training officer might further exacerbate his racism. The police policy and procedures manual states that all sexual harassment complaints are to be filed with the head of personnel and training, who happens to be Captain Irene Jamison. You would have to go over her head, and she answers to the chief of police. You've only met him briefly on two occasions. He is also a white guy who could harbor prejudice against African Americans, plus he probably wouldn't do anything because of Jamison's husband being on the city commission. You wonder if you should jeopardize the job you worked so hard to get or jeopardize your family and your values.

Based on what you have read, answer the following questions:

1. What are the basic legal requirements for a case of sexual harassment? Review some agency policies in your area and indicate what elements must be present to justify a charge of sexual harassment. Does the scenario fit the definition?

2. This scenario is not a typical case of sexual harassment. There are gender-role, cultural, and political issues present. Discuss some of these issues and indicate why they could be a problem for you.

3. List all the options you have. What are the consequences of each option? Which option would you choose and why?

CASE 8

THE TRANSMISSION OF JUSTICE

"If there is anything you can do to help, Officer Jenkins, I would really appreciate it."

After assuring Mr. Arnaud you would see what you could do, you hang up the phone and stare out of the window, watching the September rain fall.

Six months ago, Mr. Arnaud's seventeen-year-old son, Tony, had been implicated in a car-stereo theft ring. As a veteran detective, it had always been your policy to divert juveniles from the justice system whenever possible and to handle each situation as informally as possible. Since there was only nonspecific hearsay evidence against Tony by one of the boys who got caught breaking into a car, you worked out a pretrial diversion arrangement with the Assistant D.A. for Tony to do two months of volunteer work at the local boys-and-girls club and to receive counseling. He agreed, and two months later his record was expunged. Tony seemed like a good kid. He made decent grades and liked to fish. You remember thinking to yourself, "A kid who likes to fish can't be that bad."

After the first snowfall, the transmission in your SUV broke down and needed repair. "Transmissions R US" had kept your truck for two weeks and had finally called to tell you it was ready. You had stopped by the credit union to do the paperwork for a short-term loan—SUV transmission work was always expensive! When you had attempted to pay the clerk for the repair, she asked you to wait for a moment. Much to your surprise, Mr. Arnaud walked into the customer courtesy lounge and extended his hand. After escorting you to the privacy of his office, he had informed you that your money was no good at his place of business. You protested mildly and offered to pay, but Mr. Arnaud would have none of it. As he walked you to your truck, he had assured you that he would write the work off. Although you had felt a little uncomfortable in accepting his generosity, you were more than just a little glad that you didn't have to take out a loan.

Now, it was payday of another kind. Apparently, Mr. Arnaud's son Tony had been found in possession of some stolen car-audio equipment.

Mr. Arnaud had called to see if there was anything you could do to help with the situation. You know the arresting officer. He is an old friend who owes you a couple of favors, and you remind yourself that you have always liked to help salvageable kids stay out of the system. Still, you don't like being squeezed by Mr. Arnaud and aren't sure diverting Tony a second time will teach him the lesson that he needs to learn. And you also feel a little guilty that you had accepted that free transmission work.

Meanwhile, Mr. Arnaud is waiting for your call.

Based on what you have read, answer the following questions:

1. Would it be tempting to accept the transmission work if you were the police officer in question? How might that compromise your professionalism? If you had not accepted the free work, would your decision change at all?

2. What if you were Mr. Arnaud? Would you do what he did the first time your son or daughter got in trouble? Why or why not?

3. Is Tony still "salvageable?" What might be the pros and cons of a second attempt at diversion?

Section VII

POLICE ADMINISTRATION AND SUPERVISION

Introduction

Police officers have many basic responsibilities and work in a variety of ways. They drive patrol cars, direct traffic, counsel juveniles, intervene in family disputes, enforce laws, write reports, interrogate suspects, interview victims and complainants, testify in court, investigate accidents, prepare budgets, render first aid, provide security checks at residences and businesses, collect and preserve evidence, give public talks, and engage in numerous other functions that come within the purview of their mission. Their duties are numerous and often conflicting.

Because police organization cannot have a separate unit to perform each of the tasks for which the police are charged, it becomes necessary to combine and administer them in some systematic way. Sir Robert Peel recommended in 1829 that the police be organized along military lines. The military is organized in a fashion that makes the most of effectiveness and efficiency theories. As a result, many police agencies have utilized military organizational theories to develop a model for police organizations. Police rank, chain of command, lines of authority, span of control, unity of command, and even uniforms are based to a large extent on the military model of organization.

Although there are many similarities between the police organization and the military, there are also many differences. The separation of the ranks in the police organization is not as diverse as in the military. Patrol officers do not have to salute lieutenants or captains in most police departments. Also, it is not uncommon to find police captains socializing with patrol officers. Most higher-ranking police officers acquired their rank by moving up from patrol officers. Police chiefs in the United States usually were once patrol officers. There is no R.O.T.C. or O.C.S. for police recruits entering the profession. Furthermore, there are few lateral transfers of officers from one department to another. For instance, a police sergeant could not expect to transfer to another police department as a sergeant (Cordner and Sheehan, 1998).

Police organizations are typically led by an elected leader. City police departments are usually under the control of the mayor or city council, while county police departments are under the control of the sheriff, and state police agencies are under the control of the governor. Of course, this does not mean that mayors and governors make detailed decisions regarding police matters. Generally, such decisions are made by officers in the department who are experienced in police matters. The highest official in the police department is usually a police chief or commissioner. The chief is responsible for running the police department and advises the mayor or city council under whom he serves.

Below the chief of police, police agencies are frequently organized into two broad divisions: line and staff. Staff services perform technical, advisory, and support services, while line services comprise the law enforcement area of the department (i.e., patrol, traffic, and investigations). Within line and staff services, specialty divisions may be formed (e.g., homicide, juvenile, patrol, jail, crime lab, etc.).

Police Chain of Command

A chain of command exists in most police departments. The chain of command is an organizational mechanism that establishes formal lines of communication within the police agency. The line of communication stretches from the chief through supervisory officers such as captains, lieutenants, and sergeants, to patrol officers and detectives. The chain of command normally means that information travels up the chain from the patrol officer to sergeant, to lieutenant, to captain, and finally to the chief. Direction and discipline flow down the chain. The chain of command is an invaluable organizational tool because it establishes formal communication links. If a police department is to be properly organized, these communication links should be used by everyone within the organization to communicate formally in any way. If the chain of command is not utilized for all formal communicating, serious organizational difficulties may arise. For example, a chief of police who disregards the chain of command by issuing orders directly to patrol officers is breaking the chain and dissipating the authority of all those within the chain who have varying degrees of authority over the patrol officers' duties. Patrol officers may quickly learn that the chain of command is inconsequential in internal communications and that they can also disregard it in their efforts to communicate upward in the police organization.

Ranking officers who neither command nor supervise line officers are usually staff personnel. Although these officers may hold rank, they usually do not have command or supervisory authority over anyone. For example, a lieutenant assigned to staff services as a crime lab technician is in a staff position, not a command-level line position such as a lieutenant in patrol division.

The Police Chief

A police chief is by far the most important planning, organizing, staffing, directing, controlling, and system-building position within a police department. Because the position of chief of police is so precarious, many chiefs try to do everything themselves, attempting to become personally involved in all aspects of the police role. Career success is not achieved, however, through interference in activities for which others have been delegated authority.

Initially, all police chiefs should be able to perform successfully the following seven organizing tasks:

1. Group similar functions within the organization to facilitate task accomplishment.

2. Construct spans of control that are sensible and designed to strengthen supervision.

3. Apply the principle of unity of command in order to develop good working relationships between supervisors and subordinates.

4. Delegate necessary authority.

5. Hold those to whom authority has been delegated fully responsible for their actions.

6. Establish a meaningful and relevant chain of command designed to enhance organizational communication.

7. Organize so that decision making and problem solving may take place at organizational levels (Cordner and Sheehan, 1998).

Police Discipline

Leadership is a most important skill for a police administrator. Qualities of leadership that induce subordinates to render their best service vary widely. Fyfe et al. (1997) point out that "superior leaders are nearly always intelligent . . . , emotionally stable and physically strong, who have contagious enthusiasm and forceful personalities that seem to reach out and grip people who come under their influence." Unfortunately, such an example of police leadership is often not reflected in many police chiefs. If these qualities were found in police chiefs, many current problems of morale and discipline within police ranks would not exist.

Most police administrators and supervisors were once police patrol officers. As patrol officers, many of these persons experienced the same temptations, corruption, violations of regulations, and unethical police practices that many patrol officers now engage in under their command. The only difference between the police administrator and the patrol officer in this respect is the administrator must discipline those officers violating regulations, if they are caught. There seems to be a wide gap between supervisors and subordinates in many police organizations. Patrol officers do "their thing" while supervisors "do theirs." In some departments this process can become a "cat and mouse game." Supervisors try to catch subordinates goofing off or in violation of department regulations while the subordinates are trying to stay one step ahead of being caught. Clearly, this is not proper leadership but is too often a common occurrence within police agencies (More, Wegener, and Miller, 2002).

In some cases, a promotion to a supervisory level for an officer increases police morale. Lower-ranking officers know the supervisor is one of them and tend to feel they have more freedom. In many instances this higher morale disappears when officers find their new supervisor adjusting to a supervisory role rather than remaining the same.

Police Unions

Police strikes are forbidden in most states and within all police agencies. However, such regulations have not deterred police unions from participating in such disruptions. Police unions are one of the primary concerns of every police administrator.

Police unions may appear legally and formally within a police organization or they may be organized informally. Typically, informal unions are organized under police associations such as the Fraternal Order of Police. In most police agencies, these unions are organized for the purpose of collective bargaining with police administrators and with local government leaders (More, 1998). Police unions are not necessarily bad, but do often come under heavy criticism because of strikes or the threat of strikes (More, Wegener, and Miller, 2002). When strikes do occur, the statement President Woodrow Wilson made during the Boston police strike of 1919 usually appears in newspapers: "A strike of policemen of a great city, leaving that city at the mercy of an army of thugs, is a crime against civilization" (Bennett and Hess, 2001).

It is important to realize that a police strike is the last possible hope for police officers seeking redress of grievances from local government officials. Police employee dissatisfaction develops from poor communication and management's lack of concern and appreciation for employees and the work they do. Such dissatisfaction does not materialize overnight, but develops slowly over a period of years. One of the first allegations police officers make when a strike is threatened is "bad faith bargaining" (More, Wegener, and Miller, 2002). Collective bargaining is a viable procedure for airing grievances and communication between management and police employees. Collective bargaining works when both parties are genuinely interested in both the welfare of the community and the needs of the workers. When this communication deteriorates to the point where one or both parties becomes disinterested in the needs of the other, bad faith bargaining is the result (McAndrews, 1989).

Not all bad faith bargaining leads to a full-blown police strike. Police officers have devised many methods for hurting their employers without striking. The "Blue Flu" is a common occurrence that falls just short of striking. "Blue Flu" usually occurs when the police department is at its busiest time with traffic or when carnivals, fairs, and concerts are in town. Police officers individually call in sick to protest management's bargaining practices. Police officers may also reduce the issuance of citations for parking and traffic violations, which deprives the local government from revenues generated by such activity. Police officers may refuse to answer all but emergency calls while on duty. This type of activity induces the community to complain to government leaders that police service is not being provided.

Police unions may have a permanent place in modern police organizations. However, police strikes and work slowdowns can be avoided if the police and management will follow guidelines such as the following ones:

1. Police and government officials should work toward developing an atmosphere of trust and cooperation important for good faith bargaining.

2. Police administrators must get politically involved in decisions made by government officials that may have an impact on the efficient operation of the police agency.

3. Internal communication between supervisors and subordinates must be developed in an effective manner.

4. Better communications and selection between the police administrator and government officials must be established.

5. Government officials and police officers must be made aware of the problems facing each other with a genuine interest in meeting the needs of the police, government, and the community (More, Wegener, and Miller, 2002).

Minority Personnel Selection

One of the tasks of administrators is to adopt nondiscriminatory hiring practices for the law enforcement agency. Traditionally, this task involved several steps to insure quality applicants for police positions. These steps include, but are not limited to:

1. Written civil service examinations
2. Psychological testing
3. Polygraph testing
4. Background investigations
5. Requirements for minimum education
6. Assessment center activities
7. Personal interviews (Bennett and Hess, 2001)

In recent years, police personnel selection practices have come under close scrutiny with respect to females, minorities, older applications, and applicants with disabilities. In numerous instances, the federal courts have found entrance tests and job qualifications to be discriminatory against these categories of police applicants (Cordner and Sheehan, 1998). Intervention by the courts have forced some law enforcement agencies to revise their application processes, to actively engage in recruitment of females and minorities, and to make job descriptions more appropriate for disabled Americans (Schneid and Gaines, 1991; Rubin, 1995). For instance, it would make little sense to require dispatchers to be sworn officers when the task could very effectively be accomplished by a disabled individual. Court intervention has sometimes required agencies to lower standards and fill quotas based on populations of minorities in the community, a practice that may be distasteful not only to police administrators and officers but also to minority applicants who may be seen as mere tokens.

Summary

Most police departments are organized on a paramilitary model. The military model of organizations can allow for an efficient and effective delivery of services.

However, the police organization is unlike the military in that the lower-ranking police officers are expected to make complicated decisions rather than just respond to orders. In view of this, it is most important that police agencies make optimum use of supervision and leadership skills. Following basic organizational principles of chain of command and lines of communication and supervision is very important if the police organization is to be efficient. These principles can also create a high degree of morale in the police agency.

The police chief or chief administrator has the ultimate responsibility for insuring that the police organization is working in an efficient and effective manner. The police chief may accomplish this task if he/she has utilized the basic principles of organizational management, delegated proper authority, and kept lines of communication open. Police unions and collective bargaining by police officers and police management has become a growing concern of many police administrators. A major concern of police administrators is the threat of police work slowdowns or strikes. These actions can be prevented if both management and police officers work together and respect each other's needs and priorities at the bargaining table.

A police agency should be a reflection of the culture and ethnicity of the community. Police administrators must insure that minorities, females, and disabled persons have opportunities to become employed within the police agency. By the same token, police administrators must insure that only qualified persons become law enforcement officers. Lowering standards to include unqualified applicants may destroy morale as well as the police image in the community.

References

Bennett, W., and K. Hess. (2001). *Management and Supervision in Law Enforcement*, 3d ed. Belmont, CA: Wadsworth.

Cordner, G., and R. Sheehan. (1998). *Police Administration*, 4th ed. Cincinnati: Anderson Publishing Co.

Fyfe, J., J. Greene, and W. Walsh. (1997). *Police Administration*, 5th ed. New York: McGraw-Hill.

McAndrews, I. (1989). "The Negotiation Process," in R. Unsinger and H. W. More (eds.), *Police Management—Labor Relations*. Springfield, IL: Charles C Thomas.

More, H. (1998). *Special Topics in Policing*, 2d ed. Cincinnati: Anderson Publishing Co.

More, H. W., F. Wegener, and L. S. Miller. (2002). *Effective Police Supervision*, 4th ed. Cincinnati: Anderson Publishing Co.

Rubin, P. (1993). "The Americans with Disabilities Act and Criminal Justice: An Overview." *Research in Action,* September. Washington, DC: National Institute of Justice.

Schneid, T. and Gaines, L. (1991). "The Americans with Disabilities Act: Implications for Police Administrators." *Police Liability Review* (Winter):4.

CASES INVOLVING POLICE ADMINISTRATION AND SUPERVISION

Our police systems often follow a more military style of organization and administration. The police officer in a command position needs to possess leadership capabilities as well as qualities that will promote morale within the department. As a result, contemporary police administrators have the responsibility to satisfy not only the needs of the community but also the needs of department members.

In the following eight cases, you will find yourself in police supervisory positions. In each case you must make a decision based on what you know from the narrative and the available resources given to you.

Case number one, "Mrs. James Thorton, III," deals with a member of the city council demanding that punitive action be taken against a police officer. The council member is threatening to turn down the police chief's request for additional salaries and equipment for the police department unless punitive action is taken against the officer. The chief finds that the officer performed his duty in the correct manner. The chief must decide what to do and how to do it.

Case number two, "Good Officer—Poor Commander," concerns a police lieutenant who has been promoted to shift commander. While having an outstanding record of achievement as a lieutenant, the commander is finding it difficult to provide effective leadership.

Case number three, "Burned-Out in Blue," describes how stress is affecting an entire department. A police lieutenant, in charge of preparing his department for an upcoming accreditation, is faced with the dilemma of convincing the chief of the department's stress problems.

Case number four, "Chain of Command," is concerned with an assistant chief of police who becomes frustrated with the chief of police. The assistant chief finds himself burdened with a great deal of responsibility but very little authority when the chief overrides several decisions.

Case number five, "Discipline," deals with a newly appointed chief who finds himself having to be an administrator rather than just one of the officers. The chief experiences conflict with the officers that are his friends and whom he must now discipline.

Case number six, "Minority Recruitment," involves a progressive chief trying to find ways to attract minority applicants to his police department.

Case number seven, "An Out-of-Shape Department," is concerned with the problem of poor physical fitness in police agencies. A chief of police must decide how he is to persuade his officers to begin and maintain proper physical fitness habits.

In case number eight, "Blue Flu," a chief of police is faced with a work slowdown and possible strike due to the Board of Mayor and Aldermen reneging on a promised pay increase. The department is the lowest-paid police department in the region.

MRS. JAMES THORTON, III

You are the chief of police in a city with a population of approximately 25,000 people. You are respected and admired by your officers. You became chief three years ago when the city council appointed you from assistant chief to fill the retired chief's post. You have always had a good relationship with the members of the city council, although a city election was held recently and two new council members were elected. You met briefly with both of the new council members at the last meeting and felt they would be supportive of your department. City council support is extremely important at this time because you are in the process of developing next year's budget for the police department.

Budget work is one area of police management for which you have not developed any affinity. It seems more and more difficult to justify and obtain funding, particularly since federal grants have become more difficult to procure. Your goal is to include a substantial salary increase for your officers as well as some additional equipment for the department in next year's budget. Apparently, the city council is pleased with the accomplishments and progress of your department and should be responsive to your requests.

While you are working on the budget proposal, your secretary advises that you have a phone call from one of the council members.

"Yes, this is Chief Phillips. May I help you?"

"You certainly may, Chief. This is Mrs. James Thorton, the third. I have a complaint about one of your officers."

Mrs. James Thorton, III is one of the new members of the city council. Mrs. Thorton married into a wealthy family in your city and is the former president of the city school board. Mrs. Thorton considers herself a socialite and projects a bit of arrogance because of her wealth and power. She has a substantial amount of influence on the city council. She indicated to you at the last council meeting that she would be supportive of your new budget proposal.

"A complaint, Mrs. Thorton? Who was the officer and what did he or she do?" you ask in a surprised manner.

"Patrolman Everett Bailey. Officer Bailey stopped me this morning next to Cedar Bluff school and issued me a ticket for speeding in a school zone. I explained to Officer Bailey that I was late for an appointment and that I am a member of the city council. He insisted on giving me a ticket anyway. I knew if I called you, you would clear this up. Doesn't your new budget proposal come up at the next meeting?" Mrs. Thorton went on.

"Yes, Mrs. Thorton. Let me check into it and I'll call you back. I'm sorry this happened. Goodbye," you respond.

Mrs. Thorton was very upset and practically threatened to veto your new budget proposal if you weren't acquiescent to her request. You decide to consult Officer Bailey for the details.

"Everett, I received a phone call from Mrs. James Thorton. She said you issued her a speeding ticket . . ." you are interrupted by Officer Bailey before you finish.

"I certainly did, Chief. That woman has been speeding through that school zone for some time. I've warned her several times, but she insists on speeding. I was working radar at the school zone this morning and clocked her at 55 mph. I stopped her and she threatened that she would have my badge and that she could speed if she desired since she was a city council member on an important errand. She became more and more obnoxious, and I issued her a citation. One of these days she's going to hit a child over there. I've got two children in that school myself," Officer Bailey explains.

"OK, Everett. You were correct in issuing her a speeding citation. Now, let me explain the problem," you say, explaining to Officer Bailey the circumstances surrounding the incident.

"Everett, I'm going to have to make a tough decision. If we fix the ticket, Mrs. Thorton will never learn to stop speeding in this city. On the other hand, if we don't we may not get the salary increase or the equipment we need next year," you explain, hoping that Officer Bailey will understand the predicament.

Officer Bailey appears puzzled.

"I don't know, Chief. If we fix the ticket, Mrs. Thorton will have no respect for us. This may happen time and again if we don't follow through this time. I'd rather we take our chances with the remainder of the city council as far as the budget is concerned," Officer Bailey reasons.

Officer Bailey is probably correct in assuming that Mrs. Thorton would have less respect for the police department. It is also true that if you fix the ticket this time there may be another ticket and another threat. Mrs. Thorton has a great deal of influence on the other members of the city council, and if she votes against your budget request a substantial number of the other board members may follow her lead.

Based on what you have read, answer the following questions:

1. What should you, as chief, do in this situation? What are your options?

2. Were you correct in checking with Officer Bailey about fixing the ticket?

3. Could the ticket be fixed without Officer Bailey knowing about it? How does overriding an officer's decision in such a case as this affect the morale of the department?

CASE 2
GOOD OFFICER—
POOR COMMANDER

You are the chief of police of a medium-sized police department. After reading an evaluation report from your deputy chief in the patrol division, you are concerned over the evaluation of the second shift patrol unit. It appears that morale is low among the officers of that shift and the unit's efficiency is down.

Three months ago the commander of the second shift unit, Captain Owens, retired. The vacant position was filled with a young lieutenant, Bob Kingston. Kingston's background is full of accomplishments. He joined the police force seven years ago when he was 21 years old. He has a Bachelor's degree in Criminal Justice and has just finished his Master's degree in Sociology. Kingston spent 18 months on patrol before he was promoted to sergeant. A year later, Sergeant Kingston was placed in the records division. Three years ago, Kingston was promoted to lieutenant and placed in charge of the communications bureau.

Lieutenant Kingston is well-educated, highly motivated, responsible, and mature. He performs every task assigned him with careful accuracy and logic. Lieutenant Kingston has increased the effectiveness and efficiency of every division bureau in which he has worked.

Seven months ago, when your department was seeking someone to fill Captain Owens' position as shift commander, you were pleased to see Lieutenant Kingston's name on the promotion list. Lieutenant Kingston received the highest score on the shift commander's written examination. He also scored high on the promotion board's oral interview.

In view of Lieutenant Kingston's past performance, high scores, and his potential, you readily accepted the promotion board's recommendation to promote Kingston to captain and shift commander.

Now, looking at the poor evaluative report of Captain Kingston's shift, you are puzzled. You decide to confer with the deputy chief about the problem.

191

"Dave, we've been looking at your evaluation on the second shift patrol. What seems to be the problem?"

"I was concerned too, Chief. The personnel bureau has had several requests for transfer from the second to another shift. Apparently, no one's pleased with the way Kingston is running the show," Deputy Chief David Pike answers.

"Just how is he running the show?" you ask, somewhat perplexed.

"By the book. Kingston is following departmental policy and regulation by the letter. Best shift commander we've ever had, as far as the paperwork goes. All the reports are accurate, neat, and detailed. I'd say his evaluation report will improve next time; after all, he's only been on the job for three months. Give him some time—he'll be all right," Pike advises.

Deputy Chief Pike's comments do not satisfy your concerns. Pike only knows what he reads about the shift's operations. Pike has already commented on the reports' accuracy and details. However, Pike did not explain the low morale of the officers on the second shift. Reports can be deceiving, and the only way to find out what is happening on the second shift is to observe. You decide to call in one of the sergeants on the second shift patrol.

"Hello, Sergeant Bellows. . . . I just thought I'd call you in to see how things are going on your shift."

"I guess you should ask Captain Kingston about that, sir," Sergeant Bellows responds.

"Well, I would, except I want to know how he is doing in his new position. Know of any problems? Don't worry about telling me; nobody's going to know about our meeting except you and me, OK?"

"Well sir, if you really want to know . . . Captain Kingston's a good officer, really knows his stuff. But he goes by the book too much—I mean, there's no flexibility. And he thinks reports are more important than our doing the jobs," Sergeant Bellows explains.

"Sergeant, why don't you give me a couple of examples."

"Well, just last week we had that armed robbery on Cecil Street. The suspects were travelling in a white sedan heading west on Clairemont in Alpha sector. We had a unit not two blocks from there in Beta sector, and Captain Kingston ordered him not to pursue because he was the only unit in Beta sector and it's against policy for a unit to leave his sector unprotected. He's also more interested in how we write our reports than how we do our jobs. Seems like he's more concerned with details than the real reason we're out on the streets. Some of the officers like to switch off-days on occasion. Yesterday, one of my patrol officers, Kim Berry, wanted to switch off-days with Tim Sheets because his daughter was in a school play; Captain Kingston refused because it's against departmental policy. Captain Owens was never that strict." Sergeant Bellows contends.

What the sergeant said about the former captain was true. Efficiency is important, but so is flexibility.

Based on what you have read, answer the following questions:

1. What should you do at this point?

2. What problems might arise if Captain Kingston continued to perform efficiently and by the book?

3. What kinds of evaluation can be utilized to identify good leaders in a police organization?

CASE 3
BURNED-OUT IN BLUE

You have been a lieutenant in charge of planning and research for a medium-sized police department for nearly five years. You joined the department twelve years ago, fresh out of college. You were one of a number of young officers hired during what has come to be known as the "transitional period." Thirteen years ago a new chief was selected, and nearly half of the officers then with the department had retired. It was a transition from a small, traditional, and predominantly older police force to one that had nearly doubled in size with a new younger force of officers. The new chief's policy regarding hiring only persons with at least two years of college and the city's annexation of large tracts of land area had dramatically changed the image of the department.

Over the past five years you have noticed a gradual decline in efficiency. At first you did not think too much about the trend concerning inefficiency, but over the past twenty-four months the decline has become much more noticeable. There have been more accidents among the officers, the quality of arrests has declined, reports have increasingly become sloppier and more incomplete, more officers have been using sick days, officer evaluation ratings are poorer, and morale among the officers seems lower than ever. You have also noticed an increase in disciplinary actions taken against officers for failing to report to work on time, negligence, sleeping on duty, and even using alcohol and drugs while on the job. Although you do not have documentation, you suspect that there has been an increase in divorce among the officers as well. In short, you are beginning to feel like your department is "going to hell in a hand-basket."

The symptoms indicate stress is increasing among the officers of your department and is affecting the quality and efficiency of police operations. When you report your suspicions to your supervisor, he reacts with disinterest and appears almost apathetic about your concerns.

"Look, we can expect a little stress to impact the operations of the department, but there's not a whole lot we can do about that right now. Let the line supervisors deal with that. After all, they're supposed to discipline their subordinates. The chief's position is, if they can't take the

194

heat, they should get out of the kitchen. You need to concentrate on that accreditation site visit coming up next year. Accreditation is our number one priority and that's your job," Deputy Chief Cronan advises you.

Accreditation is important, but it requires the department to be at full operating strength. Every officer in the department has to work together to ensure that the stringent police accreditation standards are met. It would be very embarrassing to you, the chief, and the city if the department were denied accreditation. You are well aware that your career would be damaged, perhaps destroyed, if accreditation were denied. After all, working on gaining accreditation is your primary job in planning and research.

Accreditation for your department is also important to the chief. He has been promising the city council and the newspapers that the department will be one of the first five police departments in the state to receive the much-sought-after accreditation. Rumor has it that the chief will be looking to move up to a new chief's job in a larger neighboring city. Having one of the first accredited departments on his resume would put him on the inside track for such a position. And your immediate supervisor, Deputy Chief Cronan, would most likely be the front runner for the chief's slot. There's even a good possibility that you would also receive a promotion.

Several weeks after your conversation with Deputy Chief Cronan, you read a new general order from the chief's office concerning officers who are "gold bricking." The order also indicates that rotating patrol shifts are to be changed from the traditional 10-days-on, 4-days-off cycle to a new 7-days-on, 3-days-off cycle. No reasons are given on the order for the new rotation, but you suspect the chief has copied the shift schedule for the police department in nearby Havendale, since the Havendale Police Department was very recently accredited. Most of the patrol officers feel the new shift rotation order is a punitive action, particularly since it was initiated in conjunction with the gold-bricking order. You do not personally agree with that line of thought, since it is not unusual for the chief to fire out general orders without much thought or consultation.

The very next day, however, another order is issued by the chief to explain that no police vehicles except for command and investigation units are to be taken home by officers. Apparently, the chief has heard complaints about officers using their vehicles for personal use.

You are supposed to meet with the chief in two weeks to discuss progress made regarding accreditation for your department. You are concerned about the amount of stress in the department and its possible effect on accreditation. You need to address the stress problem with the chief but are unsure how to go about getting his support. Two weeks will pass before you know it—and who knows how many new orders will be issued between now and then? You are not sure if you can wait two weeks. Stress, officer performance, and accreditation are tied together in a number of ways. But how can you get the chief to listen . . . and act on that knowledge?

Based on what you have read, answer the following questions:

1. Why might a mid-level administrative lieutenant experience more stress than a higher-level police executive?

2. What are some administrative changes (e.g., shift rotation) that could improve officer morale and performance?

3. How might you approach the chief to gain his support for programs that would both satisfy his needs and help the line officers?

CASE 4
CHAIN OF COMMAND

As you step into your office to begin the day's work, you notice a pile of reports and memorandums stacked on your desk. Seeing the mountain of paperwork produces a sickening feeling in your stomach. In addition to your administrative duties of running staff services with its many daily problems, you are expected to review and disseminate stacks of reports and memoranda. Being an assistant chief of police takes more of your energy now than it did twenty-two years ago when you joined the police force as a patrol officer. You were younger then, and twelve-hour shifts and six-day work weeks did not seem to bother you. Now, however, life is different. You are an assistant chief of police in charge of 185 people in staff services.

It took you nineteen years to work your way up from patrol officer to assistant chief. Your accomplishments are satisfying; promotions were earned through performance rather than political maneuvers. The only other assistant chief, Richard Hall, became assistant chief last year when Brad Mason became chief of police. Mason and Hall had been longtime friends and were partners in patrol twenty-six years ago. Hall is nothing more than a yes-man to the chief. Hall has never been a good leader, administrator, or planner but had the right contacts to get promoted. Chief Mason, on the other hand, is well educated and ambitious. Mason will probably run for mayor in a future election.

Chief Mason is a good planner and organizer but lacks leadership qualities. Mason tries to be the good guy of the department to satisfy his own ego. He generally leaves the dirty work of discipline and personnel problems up to his subordinates. More frequently than not, their tasks have fallen into your hands.

Chief Mason has never been a close friend of yours. He probably recognizes that you have the leadership and administrative qualities he and Hall lack. It is probably the reason that he has maintained you in your position.

Sipping a cup of coffee and checking over your calendar for the day, you notice there is a staff meeting at 10 A.M. You cringe at the thought of another staff meeting. Staff meetings are held once a month with all the police executives, including the chief. Usually, staff meetings last for two hours and accomplish little. Apparently, staff meetings are the chief's way of holding the reins on the departmental activities. You look at the stack of paperwork and realize that you will have to work overtime to clear up the important tasks, since two hours will be lost in the staff meeting. Disgusted, you gather up your notes for the meeting.

Walking into the conference room, you greet the police administrators gathered around the table joking and drinking coffee. At five after ten Chief Mason and Rick Hall walk in the conference room together. Mason always likes to walk into the staff meetings late. It's his way of demonstrating his power. Hall shadows his every move. An audible chuckle escapes you as you imagine Chief Mason turning a sharp corner and breaking Hall's nose.

The first ten minutes or so are generally spent with the chief telling the gathered members old jokes and memories of past endeavors.

"Now, I guess we should get down to some serious business. Chief Hall, please fill us in on how your people are doing in line services," the chief mutters while lighting his pipe.

"We've had no problems in patrol or the detective's division this month. Had one officer resign in juvenile bureau to take a job with human services in the city as a counselor. Nothing else has happened," Hall responds.

"Human services? Ha, wants to be a social worker, does he?" the chief laughs, and everyone follows suit.

"OK, how's staff doing?" Chief Mason glances in your direction.

You pull out your notes and begin to highlight the activities of the records, jail, planning, and other bureaus and divisions under your command. Glancing around the room, you can see that your statements on the statistics you have prepared are not receiving much attention.

"At any rate, I've prepared a monthly report detailing the activities of the staff services, and I will give each of you a copy for your review and comments," you state, trying to finish up.

"That's fine. Oh, by the way, just a couple of things I need to fill you in on. I told the chief jailer to get rid of those two TVs for the prisoners. We're running a jail, not a Holiday Inn," the chief laughs, as everyone else echoes his sentiments.

"Excuse me chief, but I authorized the prisoners to have two TVs from the property room. I told the trustees that if they would paint and clean the cell blocks, they would be allowed to watch TV. They've done a good job, and there's nothing for them to do in their leisure time. I feel that in order to alleviate some of the stress and boredom they might be more manageable watching . . ."

"No TV," Chief Mason interrupts. "They're here to be punished. They can watch TV over at the county jail but not while they're here. Let 'em read those law books we had to put there for them," he adds, chuckling to himself.

You reluctantly acknowledge his order. You wish he had explained this to you before you made the authorization for the TVs. Now you are going to look bad in the eyes of the prisoners and your subordinates in the jail division.

"Another thing I should mention to you. Captain Joe Reynolds in records has requested a transfer into planning and research. There's only a lieutenant over the planning and research bureau and we've got two captains in records, so I approved the transfer. Joe's a good guy, known him for years," Chief Mason advises you.

"Chief, I refused that request for transfer. We don't need a captain in planning. Besides, Lieutenant Watts is a trained specialist in statistics and grants management. If we put Captain Reynolds over him it will decrease the efficiency of that unit. Captain Reynolds doesn't have any background in grants management," you argue.

"Well, he's got the rank and he's been in that records room so long now he's beginning to look like a file cabinet," the chief laughs, as the others in the room follow his actions.

It has been three weeks since the staff meeting. You are still frustrated with the chief's overriding your decisions, but this is how your job has been since Mason became chief. Mason enjoys running the department when it is convenient. He leaves all the responsibility to his subordinates and blames them when things go wrong.

The intercom line on your desk phone buzzes. It is Chief Mason.

"Thought I'd better tell you that Lieutenant Watts in planning threatened to quit if Captain Reynolds didn't go back to records. I told Reynolds to tell him to quit if he didn't like the way things were being run around here. You'd better go down there and see what business there is to take care of. You know, Reynolds doesn't know too much about research and I told him you would come down and help get things straightened out."

After the chief is through, you stare at the intercom. You think to yourself, nineteen years of police service is a long time. Maybe too long. With a sigh you lean back in your chair. There must be some way to straighten this mess out.

Based on what you have read, answer the following questions:

1. Draw an organizational chart of this police department.
2. Define chain of command, unity of command, and span of command.
3. What are the administrative problems with this department, and how could you cope and/or handle these problems?

CASE 5
DISCIPLINE

You have been chief of the Fulton City Police Department for nearly three weeks. You were appointed chief by an emergency meeting of the city council after the former chief and several of his administrative officers resigned. The resignation of the former chief and his aides came after several months of a state attorney general's investigation of illegal activities within the police department. Recognizing you as an honest individual, well liked, and respected by the community as well as your officers, the city council has asked you to become the chief.

You have been with the Fulton City Police Department for over 12 years, with nine years as patrol sergeant. The offer was shocking, since the jump from sergeant to chief is a rare occurrence in your profession. You eagerly accepted the offer, not merely for the status but because you felt you knew the problems and could handle the administration better than any of the other thirty-two officers in the department.

It has taken three weeks for you to adjust to your new position. Much of your time was spent reorganizing and rescheduling shifts due to the recent "loss of human resources." A meeting was held with all your officers the day you took the office as chief. You conveyed that no promotions would be made until the department "got back on its feet." You urged all the officers to work together until you could identify those officers with leadership qualities and make appropriate promotions. When you informed the officers to put forth extra effort in the performance of their duties for evaluative purposes, they seemed especially pleased that they would all have a chance to show what they could do. You've gotten along with most of the department and tried to be a friend to everyone. The improvement in the department's atmosphere was apparent in contrast to that in times of the former management. The morale of the department seems higher than it has been in quite some time. All the officers are friendly and courteous and appear eager to assist in the many administrative tasks that have befallen you.

Several of the officers who have been close friends over the years have hinted to you about their promotion. Apparently they assume their friendship will carry a great deal of weight regarding promotions.

When you took the chief's job, the thought of promoting your friends into these positions occurred to you. You know these officers well and know they would be loyal to you. Now, you are looking at these same officers and wondering how effective they would be as administrators. You realize that many of your friends in the department would be poor leaders.

Take John Cupp, for instance. John has been sergeant for seven years and is about the same age as you. John has been a close friend for over eight years. He has recently been hinting about his promotion to assistant chief. You like John but are aware of characteristics that would render him an inadequate leader in that particular position.

Some of your other friends on the force are also hinting to you about being promoted to lieutenant and captain. Apparently everyone thinks they know who will be promoted. The officers have apparently accepted the idea that you will promote only individuals who have been your friends. This has not seriously affected the morale of the officers since everyone on the force considers you to be basically a "good guy."

Being promoted to chief was a big break for your career, and you want to do the best possible job. You are aware of several other officers in the department who have education and leadership qualities that surpass your friends' capabilities. If you were to make the department as effective and efficient as you could, you would have to promote only the individuals who were most qualified. You wonder what the negative effects would be if you promoted those officers who deserve it most.

Several of the officers are beginning to become disorganized and less structured in their duties. The officers still call you by your first name and are not as respectful as they should be of your new position. Some of the officers have even disobeyed minor directives and departmental policies. Even your best friend, John Cupp, has told the other officers that they can disregard orders from the previous administration concerning procedures.

"Look, John, we can't tell the officers they can ignore departmental policy. You've already told them they can go on high-speed chases, carry whatever handgun they want, leave their assigned beats, and numerous other contradictions of policy. We must, for the time being, continue these policies and enforce them," you explain to Sergeant Cupp.

"Hey, wait a minute. We haven't done anything that you haven't done before you made chief. You used to say all the time how screwed up those directives and policies were. Remember when you used to tell me what you would do if you were chief? Well, here's your chance, partner," Sergeant Cupp answers.

You remember your previous boasts all too well. Now life is different. It's time you made some tough decisions.

Based on what you have read, answer the following questions:

1. Describe yourself in the position of new chief. What kind of person are you? What kind of sergeant were you? Are you having a role conflict as the new chief?

2. What should you do at this point? Should you have performed differently from the first when you accepted the chief's position? If so, how?

3. Can the chief of police in any size department be friends with subordinates?

CASE 6
MINORITY RECRUITMENT

You are the chief of police of a medium-sized police department located in the southeastern region of the United States. Stewartsville has a population of just over 63,000 and is situated in a rural area of the state. A similar sized city, Upton, is twenty miles away and has a state university with a criminal justice education program offering bachelor's and master's degrees. This is a benefit many of your officers have taken advantage of, particularly since you established a tuition fee waiver program for your officers two years ago.

You came to Stewartsville as chief just over five years ago. You had previously held the position of commander with the state highway patrol. You were chosen as chief of Stewartsville, replacing a retiring chief who had worked for the police department all his life. The fact that you were an outsider brought a great deal of suspicion and antagonism from many members of your department. You were, however, able to quickly gain acceptance as a fair and progressive administrator by department members, as well as the citizens of Stewartsville.

In the five years that you have been chief, you were able to gain accreditation for the department, increase salaries for officers, increase training opportunities, provide additional equipment and take-home cars, and provide opportunities for officers to further their education. The city council has, for the most part, been very supportive of your department in providing funding. Increased funding was provided mainly from newly annexed areas around the city. In fact, annexation has enabled you to increase your police force by 30 percent.

When you became chief five years ago, the only females on the force were one dispatcher, two file clerks, and one secretary. There were no sworn female officers. The attitude of the majority of the department was that females had no place in police work. The old chief indicated that it was because wives of the officers did not want their husbands riding around with a female partner. Almost immediately you were able to hire three highly qualified female officers for the department. It took several months for the department and the community to get used to female officers, but they were eventually tolerated, if not accepted, by many of the old-style officers on the force. Already one of the female officers has achieved the rank of sergeant, and another has been working in the detective division for over two years.

One problem has been minority recruitment. Stewartsville has a 10 percent African-American population that has traditionally occupied a residential area in the southeastern part of the city. While there have been relatively few racial incidents in Stewartsville, it remains a traditional southern town with a predominantly white leadership in local government as well as in private employment. The fact that the police department had no minority employees prompted a court order six years ago for the city to actively engage in recruitment of minority applicants. Thus far, that is all you have been able to do—actively recruit. No qualified applicants have come from the minority population since you have been chief. Your active recruitment has consisted of calling the university at Upton to recruit minorities graduating from the criminal justice program there.

"Professor Smith, this is Chief Davidson over in Stewartsville."

"Hi, Chief. Let me guess. You're looking for minorities to apply for a police position again," Professor Smith answers.

"Right. I know I keep calling, but we can't seem to get anyone interested in our department. I've even sent officers over there to talk in your classes, trying to encourage minorities to apply," you explain.

"I know, Chief. But you're not alone. We get calls and recruiters from all over the tri-state region looking for minority applicants. And you know, many of the other departments offer a better salary and benefits package than Stewartsville," Professor Smith replies.

That has been the main problem. Stewartsville P.D. cannot compete with other larger departments and agencies seeking minority applicants. You tried recruiting from your own city's residential minority population but found that, by the time they had graduated high school, most were interested in pursuing vocations other than police work. The only applicant that was interested could not meet minimum qualifications for education and failed the background investigation due to a criminal history.

You must come up with a plan that will attract qualified minorities to come to work for the Stewartsville P.D. without having to spend a great deal of money. The city council has been supportive, but they will only go so far. Plus, you will have to be cognizant of how the other officers on the force accept minorities. If you lowered standards just to hire minorities, it would not be fair to the other officers and, eventually, wouldn't be fair to the minority individuals who had to work under such a stigma.

Based on what you have read, answer the following questions:

1. What are some of the problems associated with minority recruitment? Explain how minority recruitment affects selection criteria for police applicants.

2. How can police administrators hire minority applicants and avoid the charges of reverse discrimination and labeling of minority officers as tokens?

3. What can you, as chief, do in terms of recruiting and hiring qualified minority applicants? Identify some immediate options and some long-range plans for future recruitment and hiring.

CASE 7

AN OUT-OF-SHAPE DEPARTMENT

You are the chief of a small-town police department. Your force of 21 officers is mainly composed of older men with a median age of 43. There is little turnover in your department and at present there are only two officers under age 30. Your town lies twenty miles from a large city. Most of the trouble your officers face comes from transients coming through your town. The primary disturbances are comprised of weekend drunk calls and family fights. You took the job as chief two years ago. You had previously worked for the district attorney as an investigator and took the chief's job as a career move. You like the idea of stepping up to a larger department as chief, but this town is nice and would not be a bad place in which to retire.

You are called to a meeting of the city council to discuss your plans for the next fiscal year and to answer any questions about your proposed budget.

"Chief, we've looked over your budget proposal and we have a few comments to make. But first we want to hear what you have to say," the mayor begins.

"I'm only asking for a 7 percent pay raise for the officers, some new equipment, a new cruiser, and one more officer for the department. I hope your comments support that," you state with a nervous grin.

"Well, we can see the need for a new cruiser. The one I've seen around town looks as though it's gone through the wringer," the mayor states.

"That's unit 8. It's got over 150,000 miles on it," you advise.

Stretching back in his swivel chair, the mayor continues, "We're concerned about the 7 percent pay raise and the hiring of an additional police officer. You know we're under a budget crunch. We've approved 5 percent across the board for all city employees. Why do you need a 7 percent increase for your men?" the mayor asks.

"They've done a good job all year and their pay scale is lower than the fire department's," you respond.

"What good job have they done?" a councilwoman asks, looking over her glasses at you from the end of the conference table.

"Well, I can bring in their activities reports so you can see for yourself if you want," you respond, not liking the tone of her voice.

"Activities? I haven't seen them do anything except cruise around town, write a couple of parking tickets, and hang out at the hamburger joint," the councilwoman replies.

"That's right, Chief. I haven't seen any accomplishments from them. They're all overweight and out-of-shape. Why, just last month a teenager beat up one of your officers. Did they ever catch that kid?" another councilman asks.

"I have heard a lot of jokes about your officers, Chief," the mayor adds. "I believe the kids call them 'McCops'?"

"Yeah. If they'd stop buying all those milk shakes at the hamburger joint, they might have enough money without the pay raise," another councilman adds. That comment brought a laugh from everyone but you.

Knowing your officers receive free meals at the hamburger joint, you decide not to respond to his comments.

"I know they're a little out-of-shape and need exercise, but they've been here a long time. We've got a state law requiring officers to meet minimum physical fitness requirements, but my officers are all 'grandfathered' in," you argue.

"Well, it's your problem, Chief. We approve a 5 percent cost-of-living raise. A new cruiser. No new employees and no new equipment for your department. I'm sorry, but that's all we can do. Furthermore, let me offer you a little friendly advice: I think the townspeople would be a lot happier with your officers if they saw them on the job more and at the table less," the mayor states; the other council members nod their heads in agreement.

Leaving city hall, you think about what the council said. It is true your officers have little community respect and apparently have little respect for themselves. Morale is low due to the low pay. Most of your officers do little more than grumble about their working conditions. You remember reading a police article about developing a physical fitness training program for officers. Your officers would never go for something like that.

Based on what you have read, answer the following questions:

1. How could you convince your officers to engage in physical fitness training?

2. What resources could you use to begin such a program?

3. What are the advantages of providing physical fitness training for police officers? How might the officers in this town benefit? What are some ways such a program could affect the opinions of the townspeople?

CASE 8
BLUE FLU

You are the chief of a police department, numbering 248 officers, that is the lowest-paid department in the region. In fact, you are the first female police chief your department has ever had. You have been with the police department for seventeen years. You had moved up through the ranks of the department to your present position as chief, where you have spent the last four years. You were promoted from deputy chief to chief by the newly elected mayor you supported during the recent campaign. There was no bitterness concerning your appointment. The former chief had resigned to accept another position, and you were highly qualified for the job. You hold a Bachelor's degree in Criminal Justice from the local university and are presently working toward a Master's degree. Realizing that the chief's position in your department is a political appointment, you are pursuing a graduate degree so that you will be qualified to teach Criminal Justice if, and when, you are ever "removed" from office.

At present, your department is going through some budgetary problems. The Board of Mayor and Aldermen has attempted to cut back on expenditures for next year. They have decided to limit salary increases to 6.5% for all city employees, including police officers.

Members of your department had attempted to obtain a substantial pay increase last year by threatening to strike. The Board temporarily resolved the problem by promising a 14% pay increase for all members of the police and fire departments, effective the following year, in order to get their pay up to the levels of other area police and fire departments. This pay raise would bring your department up to the regional average. Apparently, the Board is backing out of this agreement by limiting all city employees' salary increases to 6.5%.

As chief, you had addressed the Board of Mayor and Aldermen about the problem of a salary increase for your officers. You reminded them of their previous commitment to your officers. The Board apologized to you and explained that there was not enough money in the budget and hat they did not want to raise taxes. In addition, the mayor reminded you in a private conversation of his support for you for the position of chief.

For several months you have attempted to pass through the Board a proposal for collective bargaining. The Board was ready to accept a collective bargaining system but was staunchly against third-party arbitration. Recognizing that the police department might attempt to unionize, the Board advised you of the state law prohibiting police unions and strikes. The Board further advised you to "pass the word" that any officer joining a police union or participating in a police strike would be terminated immediately.

Collective bargaining is a good system, as long as both the administration and labor act in good faith. Realizing that the Board of Mayor and Aldermen is not receptive to the problems in your department, without third-party arbitration collective bargaining may be ineffective in meeting your department's needs.

After hearing that the Board is refusing the 14% pay increase, members of your department organized themselves within the local chapter of the Police Association. Several leaders of the Police Association attempted to bargain with the Board at the last meeting. The Board refused to recognize or hear grievances from the Police Association. The Police Association leaders defined the Board's actions as "not in good faith" and threatened to strike. The Board harshly reminded the Police Association leaders that any officer who attempted to strike or unionize would be terminated. You realized that you are about to face a major test of your leadership abilities.

Three days later, you receive an early morning telephone call at your home.

"Chief, sorry to call you so early, but we've got a problem."

The caller is Deputy Chief Waller, commander of the graveyard shift.

"Chief, almost everyone on the day shift is calling in sick. It's 6:30 now, and not one officer has shown up for work," Waller comments.

The day shift begins at 6 A.M. and ends at 2 P.M. There are 67 officers who are supposed to work day shift. Waller explains that only a few high-ranking officers have shown up for work.

"I'll be right in," you tell Waller, an uneasy feeling growing in your stomach.

While driving in to headquarters, you hear on your police radio that members of the fire department are also calling in sick. You are not prepared for this type of action. You are aware that the Police Association held a meeting two days earlier to discuss the problems with the Board of Mayor and Aldermen, but apparently you are unaware of the total results of this meeting.

Deputy Chief Waller meets you as you walk into your office.

"Chief, only five patrol officers have shown up for work. We've got a total of 12 officers working the day shift, which includes all higher-ranking officers," Waller explains.

"We'll have to call in all off-duty and vacationing officers," you tell Waller.

"Already tried that. Everyone has been saying that they are going to call in sick until the Board of Mayor and Aldermen grants them the 14% pay increase," Waller advises.

"How long can they do that?" you ask, wondering if what the officers are doing is legal.

"I've figured it up, Chief. According to our policy, an officer can—provided he or she has enough sick days built up—call in sick for seven consecutive days without a doctor's excuse. Tabulating the number of sick days the officers have built up, we'll average a 75 to 80% loss of strength for the next few days and there's nothing we can do. This city's going to be a mess without police protection for seven days," Waller comments.

You have a crisis on your hands. The dispatcher's office has called to advise you that there are no officers to answer calls for service. You know you must call the Mayor and advise him of the situation. You also know that you are responsible for the police department's operations. Something must be done. As if it weren't difficult enough to focus your thoughts, your tearful 18-year-old chooses this moment to call you on your cell phone, saying she really needs to talk to you about her breakup with her boyfriend.

Based on what you have read, answer the following questions:

1. You as chief are concerned about the welfare of your officers. Is it your responsibility to "fight" for benefits before a city council (i.e., collective bargaining agreements)?

2. What forms of collective bargaining exist? Why are there laws prohibiting unionizqation and strikes? Do these laws work?

3. What options do you have open to you? Can you fire the officers? What would the city council tell you?